Rochester and Colgate

THE UNIVERSITY OF CHICAGO PRESS
CHICAGO, ILLINOIS

THE BAKER & TAYLOR COMPANY
NEW YORK

THE CAMBRIDGE UNIVERSITY PRESS
LONDON

THE MARUZEN-KABUSHIKI-KAISHA
TOKYO, OSAKA, KYOTO, FUKUOKA, SENDAI

THE MISSION BOOK COMPANY
SHANGHAI

RECENT WINTER VIEWS OF HISTORIC EARLIER BUILDINGS
OF THE UNIVERSITY OF ROCHESTER

(1) Street scene showing on the left the building erected in 1826 for the United States Hotel, which in 1850 became the first building of the University of Rochester. (2) Part of the rear of the building showing "wing." (3) Anderson Hall. (4) The President's House. (5) Sibley Hall. (6) Observatory and Reynolds Laboratory, with Anderson and Sibley halls in the distance.

Rochester and Colgate

Historical Backgrounds of the Two Universities

By

JESSE LEONARD ROSENBERGER
Author of *Through Three Centuries*
The Pennsylvania Germans, Etc.

The University of Chicago Press
Chicago

COPYRIGHT 1925 BY
THE UNIVERSITY OF CHICAGO

All Rights Reserved

Published April, 1925

Composed and Printed By
The University of Chicago Press
Chicago, Illinois, U.S.A.

PREFACE

With respect to the University of Rochester there would seem to be a special desirability of having at this time a somewhat full account of why and how it was founded. One reason for this is that the year 1925 marks the seventy-fifth anniversary of its founding, directing attention anew to that event of 1850. Another reason may be seen in the great expansion which the University is undergoing. Both of these things, as well as perhaps others, tend to make measurably detailed information about the origin of the University of particular interest now, and tend to make it more than ever important that such information should, without any further delay, be put into a convenient form for preservation and future reference.

The roots of the University of Rochester penetrate deeper and spread wider than is commonly supposed, while those of Colgate University, which are of related interest, clearly run comparatively far back in the history of higher education in America.

Moreover, the founding of each of these two universities was the achievement of the applica-

PREFACE

tion of high altruistic purposes, prolonged and arduous efforts, and great self-sacrifice, which cannot too often be called to mind, and when recalled should add to the regard that is had for either one or both of the universities.

JESSE LEONARD ROSENBERGER

CHICAGO
March, 1925

CONTENTS

CHAPTER	PAGE
I. Rochester	1
II. Madison University	23
III. Removal Project	46
IV. University of Rochester	99
V. Founders of the University of Rochester	145
Index	167

CHAPTER I
ROCHESTER

From its earliest days Rochester, New York, has been an increasingly attractive place. As it developed, it became looked upon as an especially important site for the location of institutions of higher education. In this respect it reached out for Madison (now Colgate) University, and, failing to get that, induced the founding in 1850 of the University of Rochester. For these reasons something of the history and the character of the city down to about that time may advantageously be reviewed here.

The growth of Rochester was so steady that, before many years after it was incorporated as a city, it was in population and general importance accounted third in rank among the cities of the state. Its population has been given as 15 in 1812; 331 in 1816; 1,500 in 1820; 4,274 in 1825; 9,207 in 1830; 20,191 in 1840; and 36,403 in 1850; while its outlook for continued growth thereafter may be inferred from the fact that, by 1920, it attained a population of 292,750.

As for the site on which the nucleus of the city

was founded, that, taken all in all, was originally very far from being prepossessing. The land was partly swampy and partly covered with trees and a tangle of underbrush. Yet there was one natural advantage at that place which was very attractive. That was the excellent water power of the Genesee River.

After seeing that water power, Colonel Nathaniel Rochester, a Virginian by birth and a man of fine character and ability, entered on November 8, 1803, with two of his friends, into a contract for the purchase, for a consideration of $1,750, of a "mill lot" of 100 acres on the west side of the river. With striking prevision, he wrote, in January, 1811, to one of his friends: "It must become a town of great business at some future period." In the summer of 1811, he subdivided a portion of the tract into lots for sale. Then, in a letter written in August, 1825, he declared: "There can be no doubt but that Rochester will be one of the greatest manufacturing places in the United States. It embraces more local advantages than any other place I have ever seen. . . . . The land for 100 miles in every direction is of the finest quality . . . . and within two miles . . . . there are at least 500 seats for water works, a great number of which are now occupied."

ROCHESTER

Next after the water power, the completion in 1812 of the construction, under legislative authority, of a bridge across the river, about where Main Street East is now built over it, tended greatly to accelerate the growth of the village. Moreover, the village was on what was to become the main route of travel to the great "West" from points east and northeast, including those of New England. Again, a great impetus was given to the development of Rochester, especially as a distributing point, by the construction through it, from Albany to Buffalo, of the Erie Canal, which was completed in October, 1825. Subsequently the building of railroads to and through the city helped to make of it a great manufacturing place.

The village was at first called the "Falls," but when it was incorporated by legislative act, on March 21, 1817, it was given the name of "Rochesterville," which five years afterward was changed to "Rochester." In 1823 it was enlarged through an annexation of territory. By an act of April 28, 1834, it was, with another increase in area, incorporated as the city of Rochester, the boundaries of which were subsequently extended at different times. While flour from its mills was its principal product it was often called the "Flour City." When it later became better known for its nurseries, floriculture, and the raising and marketing of seeds, the designation became "Flower City."

Buckingham said, in his *Travels in America* (1838):

"If English towns of the same amount of population are examined for comparison with the Rochester of America, in none of them will there be found more of commercial industry, more of general competency, nor so many institutions for the promotion of knowledge, morals, and religion; while in the sobriety of its population, and in the absence of theaters, taverns, dramshops, it far surpasses them all; and in twenty years hence it bids fair to possess double its present wealth and population.

"One of the most powerful agents in producing this prosperity in Rochester, next to the fertile lands by which it is surrounded, and the water power which its river affords, has been the Erie Canal, which, passing immediately through the town and over the Genesee River by a noble aqueduct, makes Rochester the emporium of the inland trade between the Atlantic and the Lakes."

A large proportion of the early settlers of Rochester came from New England and gave to the city very much of a New England character. At first most of them applied themselves strenuously and almost exclusively to establishing some kind of business or to working in some way to provide homes and the necessaries of life for themselves and their families. They had little time or inclination to frequent places of amusement, and the latter did not as a rule thrive in Rochester, in early days.

Under "Places of Amusement," the city directory for 1844 gave: "The Museum," established in 1826, located on Exchange Street, and said to contain upwards of 100,000 curiosities; "Theater—Old Concert Hall," a hall in Child's Building on Exchange Street. This hall had been remodeled and was used some portions of the year for theatrical exhibitions. "Although less extensive than many buildings used exclusively for such purposes in other places, yet the accommodations correspond well with the encouragement given by our citizens to entertainments of this character," the chronicler said, and added that, when not occupied as a theater, the room was used for exhibitions, concerts, lectures, etc. "Reading-Room—Libraries," i.e., the reading-room and library of the Young Men's Association and the library of the Mechanics' Literary Association, all on State Street, were mentioned next, with the statement that there were also libraries in each of the seminaries and in the sixteen public schools, and that there were parish libraries connected with most of the churches. Then there was the "Rochester City Garden," on Main Street, nearly opposite North Street, described as being "filled up with saloons and arbors" in which refreshments were kept, having fireworks at stated periods, and being "a place of much resort during the summer months." After that, attention was directed to "Mount Hope Botanic Garden and Nursery," located on South St. Paul Street (as what is now South Avenue was then called), north of the cemetery, and set forth as having at the entrance a saloon where refreshments could be procured at all seasons, an extensive flower garden fronting upon the street, and "a sort of labyrinthine walk" to a "magnificent greenhouse." Last listed was "Mount Hope Cemetery." Concerning this, it was said in part: "Mount Hope is the pride of Rochester. . . . . Strangers and others visiting western New-York should not fail of paying Mount Hope a visit."

In the *Rochester Daily Democrat* of July 1, 1847, it was said, "A traveling correspondent of the *Syracuse Star* indulges in the following reflections upon the city of Rochester and its inhabitants:

"'Rochester is not only a thriving, but a business city. The fertile and the richly settled country around, her numerous manufacturing and milling establishments, and her enterprising and intelligent population, combine to give Rochester an importance in a business point of view surpassed by few cities in the eastern part of the state. Between sundown and nine in the evening, Main Street, from State to the east side of the river, presents a fair and full miniature of Broadway in New York, by the throng of people passing to and fro. So dense is the crowd that one is compelled to elbow his way along the best he can.

"'I noticed several fine blocks of buildings being constructed in different parts of the city. . . . .

"'There is less show of expensive equipage and foolish style of living in Rochester than in any other place of the size within my knowledge. . . . . There is . . . . an excellent state of society in which intelligence rather than wealth is the standard. Living is not expensive, but on the contrary within the means of all. . . . . Such a state of things, with so many elements of prosperity as Rochester contains, cannot fail of making it a place of commanding importance and desirable location. . . . .'"

Passing to the year 1849, there were then, among what the directory for 1849–50 of the city of Rochester set forth as the salient features of the city, two plank roads: the Brighton Plank Road and the Rochester and Charlotte Plank Road. The

Brighton Plank Road Company, the directory said, was organized in December, 1847, and had a capital of $16,000. The road was $3\frac{1}{8}$ miles long, partly double-track with gravel in the center. It commenced in the eastern termination of Main Street and extended to Allen's Creek, was called "East Avenue," and was "a favorite drive for our citizens." The Rochester and Charlotte Plank Road Company was organized in 1848, and had a capital of $70,000 and $5\frac{1}{2}$ miles of plank road.

There were two railroads, both of which were chartered in 1836, namely, the Tonawanda Railroad, having $43\frac{1}{2}$ miles of road, and the Auburn and Rochester Railroad, with 78 miles of road. By 1842 there were connecting lines of railroad extending from Albany to Buffalo, through Rochester.

Six banks, which were organized between 1829 and 1847, indicated the growing wealth of the city.

Thirty-five religious societies were scheduled as being in the city in 1849. They were: 5 Presbyterian (1 of them German); 1 Old School Presbyterian; 1 Reformed Presbyterian; 1 Associate Reformed Presbyterian; 2 Congregational; 4 Baptist (1 of them African); 1 Free Baptist; 7 Methodist Episcopal (including 1 German and 2 African); 3 Episcopal; 1 Universalist; 1 Unitarian; 4 Catholic (2 of them German); 1 German Evangelical Lutheran; 2 Friends (1 orthodox, 1 Hicksite); and 1 of Advent Believers.

The educational institutions in Rochester in 1849 were classified by the directory as "seminaries" and "common schools." Under the latter heading it was said that the city was divided into fifteen school districts and, in addition, had a school for colored children embracing the entire city; that the schoolhouses cost over $40,000; that the majority of them were of brick, and were "not at all inferior to many of the academies of this state." The "seminaries" were: Rochester Collegiate Institute, incorporated in 1839; Seward Female Seminary, established in 1835 and incorporated in 1839; Rochester Female Academy, incorporated in 1837; Allen Street Seminary, "instituted" in 1847; and Mrs. Greenough's Seminary.

The directory listed also, as a "Literary Association," the Rochester Athenaeum and Mechanics' Association, which, it stated, was formed in 1847 by a union of the Rochester Athenaeum, incorporated in 1830, and the Mechanics' Literary Association, incorporated in 1839.

There was no free high school in Rochester in 1849, nor until 1857, although from 1830 there was agitation at times for the establishment of one, and it was provided in the city's charter of 1834 that

ROCHESTER AND COLGATE

"high schools may be created." However, there was incorporated in 1827, and established largely by the aid of taxation, a sort of private academy, called the "Rochester High School," for "instructing youth on the system of Lancaster or Bell, or according to any other plan of elementary education." It finally became, or was in some way merged in or succeeded by, the "Rochester Collegiate Institute."

Various other cases of incorporation which are to be found in the session laws are now of interest mainly for the indications they contain of a desire on the part of prominent citizens to promote some form either of academic or of higher education. For instance, an act was passed in April, 1828, incorporating the "Rochester Institution of General Education," which should "not engage in any other business than that of encouraging and promoting education." Eleven of the leading citizens of Rochester were named as incorporators and were included, with seven other equally notable men, in the list of first trustees. Frederick Whittlesey was one of those incorporators and trustees, and the first secretary. William Pitkin was one of the trustees added later.

Four years after that, and two years before the city was incorporated, the "Rochester Institute of

ROCHESTER

Practical Education" was incorporated. Its object was declared to be "the cultivation of all the branches of a literary and scientific education, in connection with a more extensive application to the practical business of life than is usual in our existing institutions, and by uniting manual labor with study, to promote vigor of bodily constitution, provide facilities whereby young men without pecuniary resources may attain an education, and to unite the advantages of a cultivated mind with the feelings and habits of a working population."

In the state of New York there were in 1845 some 175 academies subject to the visitation of the Regents of the University of the State of New York. The Regents also listed, as subject to their visitation, and as reporting to them: Columbia College (founded as King's College in 1754), Union College (founded in 1795), Hamilton College (founded in 1812, at Clinton), Geneva College (now Hobart, founded in 1822), and the University of the City of New York (founded in 1831).

The Regents of the University of the State of New York were created in 1784, by the same act which changed the name of King's College to Columbia College. On account of the limitations which the legislature was for many years disposed to place on the amount of real and personal property that an educational institution chartered by it might lawfully hold, and the requirements as to endowments made by the Regents in 1850, it is interesting to note that in 1784 it was provided that the Regents of the University of the State of New York might hold and possess estates "to the annual amount of forty thousand bushels of wheat." Also that "if it should so happen that any person or persons, or any body politic or corporate, should at his or their expense found any college or school, and endow the same with an estate, real or personal, of the yearly value of one thousand bushels of wheat, such school or college shall on the application of the founder or founders, or their heirs or successors, be considered as composing a part of the said University." It may be added that The University of the State of New York, as it is now legally styled—omitting the words "Regents of"—is in the nature of a department or agency of the state for supervising public education, including very largely the chartering and the overseeing of academic, collegiate, and professional educational institutions; it is itself not what would be termed a teaching institution.

Since most colleges of a general character primarily and principally serve local areas, and give a certain cultural distinction to the communities in which they are located, the establishment in the nineteenth century of colleges very frequently followed close on territorial development; and one was wanted comparatively early for western New York, west of Geneva. Evidence of this is furnished by the incorporation, in 1836, of "The University of Western New York," to be located at Buffalo. A good start was made toward establishing that University, but the undertaking was rendered futile by the panic of 1837.

Ten years after that incorporation, or in 1846, the petitions of sundry inhabitants of Monroe County, of Cayuga County, of Allegany County, of Genesee and Livingston counties, and of Orleans County, were, respectively, on February 2, 5, 7, 19, and March 13, presented to the Assembly praying for the incorporation of a college or a university to be located in the city of Rochester, the petition from Cayuga County asking for it "for the aid of agriculture." These petitions were referred to in the *Journal of the Assembly*, under date of February 20, as "the petitions of sundry inhabitants of western New York." Likewise, petitions of inhabitants of Palmyra, of Yates County, and of Ontario County were, on February 9, 13, and April 9, presented to the Senate, asking respectively, according to the *Journal of the Senate*, "for a university at Rochester," "for a charter for a university of learning, etc., at Rochester," and "for the passage of a law incorporing the Rochester University."

On May 8, 1846, "An act to incorporate the University of Rochester" was passed. It named as incorporators, and to be the first trustees of the corporation: Addison Gardiner, Henry Dwight, Leonard E. Lathrop, Albert G. Hall, James [B.] Shaw, William M. Oliver, James S. Wadsworth, Nathaniel W. Fisber [Fisher], Harman [Harmon] Camp, Albert H. Porter, Phineas L. Tracy, John B. Skinner, Asa T. Hopkins, Samuel Luckey, Moses Chapin, Henry E. Rochester, E. Darwin Smith, Charles M. Lee, Enos Pomeroy, and Selah Matthews. Apparently about one-half the number were residents of other places than Rochester. Of those whose names are to be found in the city directory of that time, Addison Gardiner was lieutenant-governor of the state and president of the Senate, and was afterward a justice of the Court of Appeals; Albert G. Hall was the pastor of the Third Presbyterian Church; James B. Shaw was the pastor of the Brick (Presbyterian) Church; Samuel Luckey was a Methodist minister who, on May 6, 1847, was appointed a regent of the University of the State of New York; Moses Chapin,

E. Darwin Smith, Charles M. Lee, Enos Pomeroy, and Selah Matthews were classed as attorneys. Henry E. Rochester was also at one time listed as an attorney, but afterward as a commission merchant.

The object of the corporation was declared to be "to promote education, and to cultivate and advance literature, science, and the arts." At the same time it was provided that: "Unless the said corporation shall organize and commence a school for instruction in literature or science, with at least two professors, besides the chancellor or president, within three years from the date of this act, its corporate powers shall cease."

This was an entirely different project from that of 1847–50, which resulted in the founding of the University of Rochester, and was promoted under wholly different auspices, the incorporators being predominantly Presbyterian, while approximately five-sixths of those of 1850 were Baptists. The first undertaking proved unsuccessful; the second, successful. Still, it is probable that the efforts that were made, principally in the latter part of 1846 and in the first few months of 1847, to establish under this charter a university in Rochester, helped to prepare the way for the movement begun by the Baptists in the autumn of 1847. Furthermore, it would seem that the demands made of the incorporators of 1846 for an institution broad in scope and liberal and non-sectarian in character, and the assurances given with respect thereto, must have had more or less influence on the Baptist promoters, who, from the first, announced a broad, liberal, and non-sectarian policy for an institution which was to be none the less of a decidedly Christian character—a policy that, in its non-sectarian features, was strongly denounced by some Baptist opponents of the promoters' plans. Therefore it may be well to consider here something of what was said and done in connection with the 1846 enterprise.

An official statement, "By order of the Board of Trustees," was made by the Executive Committee on October 19, 1846. It was addressed "To the Citizens of Western New York," and was published, under the heading of "University for Western New York," in the Rochester *Daily Democrat* of November 23, 1846. It said:

"The need of a well-endowed university, affording the best possible facilities for an extended education on liberal principles, and located centrally in western New York, has for some time past been apparent. About two years ago several gentlemen, from various counties in this part of the state, met at Rochester for consultation and to adopt measures to attain this desirable object. The result of such meeting was an application for a charter, which was granted at the last session of the legislature, for an institution to be styled 'The University of Rochester.' . . . .

"At a recent meeting of the trustees, held in the city of Rochester, it was resolved that measures be immediately taken to obtain subscriptions for the endowment of the University, and that $120,000 be deemed necessary to begin efficiently and successfully the enterprise. . . . .

"As a part of the plan of the institution, instruction will be imparted in some of the more practical sciences to those who may not desire to pursue a collegiate education. . . . . There will also be law and medical departments. . . . . Finally, the trustees deem it incumbent on them to state that the plan of the University, contemplated by the charter and the measures of the board, aims to preserve the institution from all local and sectarian influences. . . . . Indeed the enlightened spirit of the age demands a liberal and united effort of all friends of religion and science in the management of our literary and other general institutions."

The *Daily Democrat* of January 11, 1847, in its account of a meeting of the citizens of Rochester which was held, on the subject of the University, at the courthouse on the preceding Friday evening, said that the chair appointed a committee of five, headed by Rev. Dr. Luckey, to draft a report and resolutions. The report emphasized that western New York needed an institution "superior in a course of instruction in the sciences requisite for the advancement of the great agricultural interests. .... The mechanics, the machinists and the manufacturers in western New York, need science .... give them science."

When a resolution was offered approving of the charter and published plan of the trustees for carrying it into effect, "as containing all the provisions essential to such an institution as the country needs; the eligibility of its location; its truly liberal and popular character, ... Rev. Mr. Holland [Unitarian] rose and spoke against the resolution in strong and energetic language. He considered the concern as narrow, illiberal, and sectarian in its character, and said that he should oppose it with all his might so long as any particular denomination had a majority in the Board of Trustees, etc."

Another resolution presented was, "That we earnestly recommend to the trustees of the University so to conduct its operations as to prevent,

ROCHESTER

as far as practicable, all occasions of suspicion that it is, or may become, sectarian in its character; not that we fear such a result, but to satisfy all who wish a truly liberal and catholic institution that they have nothing to apprehend on this account."

"An adjourned meeting," the *Daily Democrat* of January 14 said, "was held at the courthouse on Tuesday evening. The attendance was large—more being present than could obtain seats. The discussion was confined almost entirely to the issue raised at a former meeting, that the institution would be sectarian in its character, and was conducted with courtesy and ability on both sides." The two resolutions before referred to, and some others of the previous meeting, were adopted.

On January 18, the same paper published a communication which stated that there were "seventeen of one denomination and three of all others on the board." Four days later, the paper reported that, at another adjourned meeting, Judge Chapin concluded an address by showing, "in a most ingenious and overpowering argument, that no sectarian influence was to be feared, and certainly not an influence arising from the Presbyterian portion of the community."

On February 24, 1847, the *Daily Democrat* contained a communication from "C. Dewey," in which he said: "The agent of the executive committee of the trustees of Rochester University has been employed for a few weeks in obtaining subscriptions for its endowment. About $15,000 have been subscribed or promised. . . . . As my agency in the case must now cease for a time at least, I have been asked to say what is the prospect of success. . . . . True, many persons of ample means have refused to subscribe, but it was clear *they meant only not just yet*."

From this time on, this university project was not often mentioned in the newspapers. But one reference to it, in the *Rochester Daily Advertiser* of July 13, 1847—in an article suggested by a notable gift to Harvard University—ended: "The progress made in securing $50,000?—'Tell it not in Gath,' lest rival cities hear it. . . . . *'Don't give up the ship.'*"

On November 2, 1847, the *Rochester Daily American* said:

"An effort was made last winter to establish a college in Rochester under the title of the 'University of Western New York' [but properly, "University of Rochester"]. To effect that desirable object a great expenditure—at least $150,000—was deemed necessary. Much labor was bestowed upon the project, public meetings were held, subscriptions solicited, and strong desire expressed, if not much hope felt, for the success of the undertaking. The result is known—has been tacitly confessed—and is not now attempted to be concealed. It was a failure."

Alvah Strong, who for many years was one of the publishers of the *Rochester Daily Democrat*, said, in his *Autobiography*, which was written about 1880 and privately printed five years later:

"All denominations of Christians had long felt that, owing to our favored location and surroundings, a college of some sort ought to be founded in Rochester. The Presbyterians had repeatedly made most strenuous efforts to plant a college here; the Congregationalists also, a few generous men offering to do liberally. But they were not properly supported. After long, persistent labor the enterprise was abandoned in despair; and finally their influence was mostly concentrated on Clinton College [Hamilton College, at Clinton]. The Methodists desired an institution of their order here, too, but they could not change their plans, as all their strength had been absorbed in their young school in Lima. The Episcopalians were also earnest for a college, but all their forces were demanded for Hobart College.

ROCHESTER AND COLGATE

"Such was the condition of things when the removal of the Hamilton schools [Madison University] to Rochester became the exciting topic; and discussion was kept up from week to week through our city press, in private circles, and in public meetings."

Before the subject of the removal plan is taken up, it will be well to consider, for the space of a chapter, something of the history—down to 1847—pertaining to Madison University.

CHAPTER II

MADISON UNIVERSITY

One hundred and sixty-two miles by railroad, east and somewhat south of Rochester, is the village of Hamilton, in Madison County, and in what is known as central New York. The first white settlers in that vicinity were of the New England type. Two of them were the brothers Elisha and Samuel Payne, men of sterling qualities, and both Baptists. The locality in which they settled was soon called Payne's Hollow, and the settlement that was formed there, Payne's Settlement, or Paynesville, but afterward Hamilton, of which Elisha Payne, in particular, has sometimes been referred to as having been the founder.

In that settlement the ideals and spirit of New England prevailed. Religious meetings were soon held in private homes, and a schoolhouse was built by 1796, after which the meetings were commonly held in the schoolhouse. A Baptist church was constituted with seven members, in November, 1796, and a Baptist meeting-house was built in 1810.

Gradually a village was formed, which was, on April 12, 1816, incorporated as the "village of

ROCHESTER AND COLGATE

Hamilton," a year before the "village of Rochesterville" was incorporated. The settlers for some distance around found Hamilton a convenient place at which to do their trading, and the village prospered in proportion.

Roads of the kind usual in that day were of course made to and from Hamilton, but they were at many times in the year almost impassable. This was partially remedied by the construction of turnpikes; and the construction of one to run from Plainfield, in Otsego County, on the east, through Hamilton and thence northwesterly to Skaneateles, was commenced in 1811. Through Hamilton was also built the Chenango Canal, which was completed in 1836, connecting the Erie Canal at Utica with the Susquehanna River at Binghamton. But it was 1848 before the plank road between Hamilton and Utica was constructed.

It was estimated that the population of Hamilton in 1847 was about 1,500. That it was not very much greater was probably largely owing to the disadvantage of the location of Hamilton after the Erie Canal and the railroads connecting Albany and Buffalo were built on routes less than thirty miles north of it. The railroad which was eventually constructed through Hamilton was not opened between it and Utica until 1870. Nor had Hamilton any special water power, as had Rochester, to attract industries, although it had Payne Brook and, at some distance away, the Chenango River, from which the valley derived the name of Chenango Valley.

As it was, education became Hamilton's paramount industry. Not only was a school established almost immediately by the first settlers, but comparatively early an academy was founded, so that in 1816—the same year that the village was incorporated—a two-story brick building was erected, the first story to be used for the district school, and the second for Hamilton Academy.

But by far the most important things done with respect to the promotion of higher education were done chiefly by the Baptists. To begin with, in 1808 the Lake Missionary Society, which was formed the preceding year in Onondaga County to do missionary work in the western part of the state, especially in the region of the Great Lakes, changed its name and location and became the Hamilton Baptist Missionary Society, under which name it was incorporated on March 28, 1817, "for the purpose of propagating the gospel among the destitute." The incorporating act, however, provided that no regulation should be made "in any wise to control the religious principles, or affect the rights of conscience of any person whatsoever." In 1825, the name of the society was again changed, this time to the Baptist Missionary Convention of the State of New York.

Meanwhile, in May, 1817, seven men met at the home of Deacon Samuel Payne to consider the need of educating young men for the Baptist ministry and the steps that ought to be taken in that part of the state toward aiding to supply the need. The result was a published general call for another meeting, to be held in Hamilton on September 24. Thirteen men attended the latter meeting and organized the Baptist Education Society of the State of New York. Then each man paid a membership fee of one dollar. The society, as one instituted "for the purpose of educating pious young men to the gospel ministry," was incorporated by a legislative act passed March 5, 1819. Power was conferred on it to make such ordinances and regulations for "the government of the seminary . . . . and conducting all their concerns" as should appear proper. "*And provided always*, That if the said society appropriate their funds, or any part thereof, to any purpose or purposes other than those intended and contemplated by this act, or shall at any time pass any law or regulation affecting the rights of conscience, that thenceforth the said corporation shall cease and be void; and also the legislature may at any time alter or repeal this act, as in their discretion shall seem proper."

It was not predetermined that the Seminary thus indirectly authorized to be established and maintained by the society should be located at Hamilton. A number of different locations for it were in fact considered, with the result that the choice fell on Hamilton, conditioned on what was deemed equivalent to $6,000 being contributed to the enterprise.

The Seminary was formally opened on May 1, 1820, in a third story which had been added for the purpose to the brick academy building, which story was taken down after it was vacated in 1823 by the removal of the Seminary into a stone building that had been erected for it on what was known as the "plain." The sole instructor in 1820 was Rev. Daniel Hascall, who in 1813 had come to Hamilton as the second pastor of the First Baptist Church, and who had, for a while, been giving instruction at his home to young men who have been accounted students of the Seminary, or, as it came to be called, the Hamilton Literary and Theological Institution. Mr. Hascall was a graduate of Middlebury College and was a man of a great deal of energy and determination. He is generally credited

ROCHESTER AND COLGATE

with having been the one whose suggestion at Hamilton started there this educational movement.

However, back of any such suggestion, it would seem probable that some credit for what was done should be given to information gained by the Baptists of Hamilton and vicinity from the proximity of the Hamilton Baptist Missionary Society. Then, whereas the Baptists generally, as plain, pious people, had been strongly opposed to a specially educated or what they frequently termed a "man-made" ministry, there was beginning to be a noticeable awakening among leading Baptists to the need of making provision, here and there, for the education, under Baptist supervision, of young men for the Baptist ministry.

Brown University had been for over fifty years the only institution of higher learning in America appreciably under Baptist auspices. Yet, good as that University was, it alone was no longer enough —and it was not enough of a theological institution —to meet all the new requirements for the Baptists of the whole country.

So the need and the perception of it led to the chartering, in 1813, of the Maine Literary and Theological Institution, which later became Waterville (now Colby) College. That Institution opened

MADISON UNIVERSITY

its Theological Department in 1818, and its Literary Department a year later.

Again, on April 15, 1817—or in the month preceding the meeting of the seven men in Hamilton and virtually two years before the incorporation of the Baptist Education Society of the State of New York—the legislature of the state, reciting that "whereas the members of an association instituted in this state for the purpose of educating pious young to the gospel ministry have petitioned for an act of incorporation, the better to enable them to attain the objects of their association," passed an act incorporating the Baptist Theological Seminary. Under this charter, the New York Baptist Theological Seminary was founded and then maintained for a while, after which it was merged in the Hamilton Literary and Theological Institution.

In 1821, Columbian College (afterward University, and in 1904 merged with other institutions to form George Washington University) was founded, in Washington, District of Columbia; and thereafter other institutions, largely or entirely for ministerial education, were established at closely succeeding intervals under Baptist auspices, both in the North and in the South.

All this showed a live, widespread, and practical

interest being taken by many Baptists in higher, and especially in ministerial, education at about the time that the Hamilton Institution was projected and later being established, which attitude elsewhere must have had its effect at Hamilton. Indeed, the preamble to the act incorporating the Baptist Education Society of the State of New York, which originated at Hamilton, was almost identical with that of the earlier act incorporating the (New York) Baptist Theological Seminary.

On the other hand, in 1849, the New York *Baptist Register*, published at Utica, in commenting on how much had been achieved in three years at Lewisburg relative to the establishment of what is now Bucknell University, said that "when a comparison is made with the uphill, laborious progress in behalf of Hamilton . . . . some thirty years ago" there was this thing to be taken into consideration:

"Hamilton was commenced under the strongest prejudices against ministerial education; comparatively few on the stage now properly appreciate them. Aspersions were cast by some of our best brethren, and nothing was more common than to hear it sneered at, as the 'minister factory.' Indeed, for years after it was in promising operation, these prejudices were mountain-high in the churches, and the columns of the *Register* had to throw out facts and arguments continually, and at first with great caution, to remove them; many a sharp rap, moreover, would it receive for its pains. The young men likewise, how often were they subjects of uncomfortable ridicule when they went out to preach occasionally, and what invidious comparisons would be indulged in regard to them by the older brethren of age and experience in the ministry! Only within a few years, in reality, has the triumph in favor of an educated ministry been generally secured. And perhaps even now a searching scrutiny would show a number still hesitating as to its actual benefits. Some grave testimony has been furnished, we think, on this point, in the meager annual August contributions of the churches, and the entire refusal and neglect of a considerable number to transmit a single cent to the treasurer."

Daniel Hascall remained an instructor or professor in, and an efficient promoter of, the Hamilton Literary and Theological Institution up to 1835, when he resigned. In 1821, he was joined in this work by Rev. Nathaniel Kendrick, who was pastor of the Baptist Church at Eaton, about three miles northwest of Hamilton, and who then went twice a week to Hamilton to give instruction in theology, until he finally moved to Hamilton. In 1836, the presidency of the Institution was tendered to Dr. Kendrick, but he did not formally accept the office. However, he performed the duties of president until nearly the end of his life in 1848. He was a man who was highly esteemed and was especially looked up to as a wise counselor. His bearing was characterized by modesty and simplicity combined with dignity.

In 1826, Deacon Samuel Payne and his wife deeded their farm of 123 acres as a gift for the use of the Hamilton Literary and Theological Institution. Thus did the latter obtain what was scenically and in other respects a choice site for a campus of generous size extending into a peaceful valley from the slope facing northwesterly of one of the hills sheltering the valley. In consequence, on a bench on that hillside, with its commanding view, have most of the buildings now occupied by Colgate University been erected; and the "Hill" is commonly regarded as one of its distinguishing features, remembered with special interest by its alumni. First of all, what was later denominated the "Western Edifice"—a stone building four stories high and 100 by 60 feet—was erected on the hillside, and opened in 1827. Next, the "Eastern Edifice," also of stone and four stories high, but

MADISON UNIVERSITY

100 by 56 feet, was built in 1834, and a stone "Boarding Hall," in 1838.

In 1829, a four years' course of study was organized. That was in 1832 extended to six years, and in 1834 the course of study was made eight years—two years for the Preparatory Department, four years for the Collegiate, and two years for the Theological Department. Then, in 1839, the Collegiate Department was opened to young men other than those studying for the ministry. These changes in the curriculum, with a continual increase in the enrolment of students, required additions to the faculty, which were from time to time made—all, too, of a high standard.

The first catalogue issued was one for 1832–33. This stated that every candidate for admission into the Seminary was required to furnish satisfactory evidence of good moral character, piety, and talents which promised usefulness in the Christian ministry. A letter of approbation from the church to which he belonged was also expected.

The Preparatory Department, the catalogue said, besides furnishing instruction to those designing to pursue a full course (or six years), was open also to such as in the opinion of the faculty might profitably pursue a shorter course. The period of their study varied, therefore, from one to two,

ROCHESTER AND COLGATE

three, four, and five years, according to circumstances.

Under the head of "Exercise," the catalogue said: "There is a workshop connected with the Seminary, where regular exercise is furnished to the students in making window sash. A sash-maker is employed to superintend the work." Expenses were given as: "Board, washing, lodging, per week, $1.00; room-rent and library *gratuitous;* tuition per annum, $16; total for the year, $58.00."

The catalogue for 1833-34 stated that the regular course of instruction then occupied six years, and that a reference to the list of studies would show that it embraced a classical and scientific course of study nearly, if not fully, equivalent to that adopted in the majority of the colleges. It had, therefore, been deemed expedient to divide the Institution into two departments, Collegiate and Theological, appropriating to the former the ordinary collegiate names of classes. Besides, provision had been made, as theretofore, for such as wished to pursue here the requisite studies for admission into the collegiate course.

This catalogue said further that the Institution was open to young men of every evangelical Christian denomination, possessing the requisite qualifications. "Candidates for admission are ex-

MADISON UNIVERSITY

amined in relation to their Christian experience, call to the ministry, studies, etc., and are expected to present to the faculty letters from the churches or pastors of the churches to which they respectively belong, furnishing testimonials of their possession of decided piety and talents which it is believed will render them useful in the gospel ministry."

But no young man, it was stated, was considered as matriculated, or a regular member of the Institution, until he had been in the Institution one term.

Under "Admission," the catalogue of 1839–40 said: "The Institution is open to young men having the ministry in view, from every denomination of evangelical Christians. . . . . The Collegiate Department is also open, under certain restrictions, to young men who have not the ministry in view."

The *Laws of Hamilton Literary and Theological Institution*, published in 1840, provided, among other things, that:

"If any student shall marry, during his connection with the Institution, he shall be dismissed."

"The members of the Institution are expected to regard the cultivation of personal piety as their primary duty, and for this object to avail themselves of all the means of religious improvement;

ROCHESTER AND COLGATE

to spend a portion of each day in private reading of the Scriptures, self-examination, and prayer; to meet by classes or otherwise, as often as convenient, for social religious exercises; to refrain from light and trifling conversation; and, in all respects, to maintain a deportment becoming those who profess godliness, and who are looking forward to the holy work of the ministry."

"The students shall assemble morning and evening in the chapel, for social worship. . . . . At morning prayers, the members of one or more of the theological classes, as the faculty may direct, shall officiate in rotation." "At evening prayers, the members of the faculty shall officiate in rotation."

"Every student shall during term-time reside in the Institution, unless prevented by sickness or other necessity." "All students are required to board in commons, except in special cases when permission to board elsewhere shall have been obtained from the faculty."

"The faculty shall have power to admit into the Collegiate Department persons who are not studying for the ministry, under the following regulations: The number of persons so admitted shall not be such as to abridge, in any way, the privileges of those students who are preparing for the ministry.

. . . . Such persons shall not be allowed to omit any study belonging to the prescribed course."

The growth of the Hamilton Literary and Theological Institution and the opening in 1839 of the doors of its Collegiate Department for the purpose of educating, in addition to "pious young men to the gospel ministry," young men not having the ministry in view presented certain perplexities. One was the need of the power, which the Institution lacked, to confer the degrees commonly conferred by collegiate institutions. Another was the ineligibility, from not having a charter as a college, to participate in the appropriations that were being made by the state to aid its colleges. But most serious of all, perhaps, was the penalty affixed by the act incorporating the Education Society to the appropriation by the society of any of its funds to any purpose other than that contemplated by said act.

These and probably other considerations led to the presentation to the Assembly of a petition by sundry inhabitants of Madison County, praying for the incorporation of a college in the village of Hamilton—the petition referred to in an entry of March 12, 1840, in the *Journal of the Assembly*. What was evidently another petition is mentioned in an entry of March 16, 1840, as one of sundry inhabitants of Madison County and its vicinity, which is best described in *Assembly Document No. 309,* a very favorable report having been made on it April 11, 1840, by the committee to which it was referred. The report stated that the petition was for the incorporation of the Collegiate Department of the Hamilton Literary and Theological Institute, which was followed by a later statement that the petitioners solicited "an incorporation of the Collegiate Department of said Seminary, under the name of 'The Hamilton University,' with all the rights, privileges, and immunities which have been granted to the colleges of this state." Afterward it is shown by a *Journal* record of April 23, 1840, that "Mr. Walker, from the select committee to which was recommitted the engrossed bill entitled 'An act to incorporate the Hamilton University,' reported that the committee had gone through said bill, made sundry amendments thereto, altered the title so as to read 'An act to incorporate the Hamilton Literary Institution,' and agreed to the same." This amended bill was passed by the Assembly (ayes, 97; nays, 00) and ordered delivered to the Senate with a request for its concurrence; but the bill was rejected by the Senate.

A renewal of the effort to secure incorporation was made in 1843. This is shown by the *Journal of*

MADISON UNIVERSITY

the Assembly for that year, which records that on January 26 the petition of sundry inhabitants of the counties of Madison, Oneida, and Chenango, praying the passage of a law to incorporate the Madison College, to be located at Hamilton in the county of Madison, was read and referred to the committee on colleges, academies, and common schools. This resulted in a bill entitled "An act to incorporate the Madison College, in the town of Hamilton." But the bill failed of passage by the Assembly (on April 8) because less than two-thirds of all the elected members voted for it, the vote being, ayes, 64; nays, 33. Likewise, on April 17, a vote on a motion to reconsider the former vote was determined in the negative.

One result of these failures to obtain a charter for a collegiate institution, and thereby the power to confer degrees, was shown by the announcement, in the catalogue for 1844-45, that "an arrangement has been made with the Columbian College, Washington, D.C., by which the degrees of Bachelor of Arts (A.B.), and of Master of Arts (A.M.), in course, are conferred upon such young men as have satisfactorily completed the course of studies in the Collegiate Department and are recommended by the faculty as suitable candidates for such honors."

Finally, "An act to incorporate the Madison University" was passed March 26, 1846. This stated that Friend Humphrey, Seneca B. Burchard, William Colgate, and their associates were "constituted a body corporate, by the name of 'The Madison University,' for the purpose of promoting literature and science."

The act appointed the following trustees of the said corporation, with power to fill any vacancy in their board, of whom nine members should constitute a quorum for the transaction of business: Friend Humphrey, Seneca B. Burchard, William Colgate, William L. Marcy, Palmer Townsend, William Cobb, Ira Harris, Henry Tower, Nathaniel Kendrick, Alva Pierce, Bartholomew T. Welch, Edward Bright, Jr., William R. Williams, Robert Kelley, Harvey Edwards, Charles Walker, Smith Sheldon, Joseph Caldwell, John Munro, John N. Wilder, George Curtis, Elisha Tucker, Pharcellus Church, James Edmonds, Joseph Trevor, Amos Graves, and Alonzo Wheelock.

"The location of the said University," the act stated, "shall be at the village of Hamilton in the county of Madison."

The granting of diplomas was authorized.

Two of the other provisions were:

"The Baptist Education Society of the State of

MADISON UNIVERSITY

New York is hereby authorized to make such arrangement with the said University for the transfer of the property of the said society, or any part thereof, either absolutely or conditionally, to the said University, as the society shall deem proper.

"The legislature may at any time alter or repeal this act."

As soon as it could well be done after Madison University was thus chartered, it was formally organized and arrangements were made by which it became the successor not only of the Collegiate Department, but practically for carrying on all the educational work at Hamilton of the Baptist Education Society of the State of New York.

The report for the year ending August 18, 1847, made by the trustees of Madison University to the Regents of the University of the State of New York, stated that the faculty consisted of Rev. John S. Maginnis, D.D., professor of evidences of natural and revealed religion; Rev. Thomas J. Conant, D.D., professor of Hebrew; Rev. George W. Eaton, D.D., professor of civil history; Rev. A. C. Kendrick, A.M., professor of the Greek language and literature; J. F. Richardson, A.M., professor of Latin; J. H. Raymond, A.M., professor of rhetoric and *belles lettres;* Samuel

ROCHESTER AND COLGATE

Graves, A.B., tutor in mathematics and natural philosophy.

Of bell-ringers there were three.

The whole number of undergraduates during the year was 136. The number of those who left during the year was 19, of whom 17 were honorably dismissed, 1 was expelled, and 1 separated from the Institution, leaving 117 at the close of the year. By classes there were: Seniors, 22; Juniors, 28; Sophomores, 43; Freshmen, 43. The number of graduates at the last Commencement was 18, having an average age of 25 years. (The catalogue for 1846-47 gave: resident graduate, 1; in Theological Department, 30; undergraduates, 144; in Grammar School, 34; total, 209.)

No individuals (the trustees said) were aided by the University board; but above fifty undergraduates were assisted to the amount of their board and tuition through the instrumentality of the New York Baptist Education Society.

"The board are allowed the use of the following articles of property belonging to the Ed. Society, viz.: Two four-story college buildings, of stone, ... valued at $10,000; furniture for students' rooms, $1,200; library of about 5,000 well-selected volumes, $8,000; philosophical and chemical apparatus, $1,500; Cottage Edifice of stone, contain-

MADISON UNIVERSITY

ing three recitation rooms, and rooms for the philosophical and chemical apparatus, $500.

"The board have, as yet, no invested fund; their reliance, at present, for the support of the University, is on private benevolence, tuition fees, and the aid of the state. The first two are the only sources which the managers of the Institution (either before or since the obtaining of the University charter) have enjoyed in sustaining it during a period of twenty-seven years. For the last fifteen years, during which there has been a full college course of study and system of education, the average annual expense of the Institution above the income from students' fees, and including what has been paid to indigent students, has been about $12,000. . . . .

"The whole amount charged for tuition, room rent, etc., during the year, was $3,162.75, of which there was collected or is considered collectible, $3,000. Contributed by the patrons of the University, $6,000. Expenditures as follows, viz.: To officers, agents, servants, etc., $8,460; library and apparatus, $300."

The price of tuition was $30.

The "whole number of graduates from college" was given as 197. Another statement made was that above 1,200 individuals had enjoyed either in full or in part the advantages of the Institution, the most of whom were engaged in fields of useful professional labor.

In connection with this report it is interesting to note, as supplemental to it, a few things stated in the report for the academic year ending in August, 1850. The latter report said that the Western Edifice contained a spacious chapel, three recitation rooms, library room, reading-room, museum, and rooms with double apartments to accommodate about fifty students. The Eastern Edifice had two neatly finished halls for the literary societies, two recitation rooms, and students' rooms with double apartments to accommodate about one hundred students. Besides those edifices and the Cottage Edifice, there were a boarding-house and two houses erected for professors. There was an income of about $500 from certain invested funds. Moreover, it was thought proper to state that in a report prepared for the Regents in the spring of 1847 (though not presented), in which the provisional committee of the University and the faculty concurred, the value of the listed property was estimated at a little over $40,000; and its value remained about the same as then, except the wear by natural use.

This outline of the early history of the village

MADISON UNIVERSITY

of Hamilton, of the development of the Hamilton Literary and Theological Institution, and of Madison University to August, 1847, or to about that time, besides being of whatever interest and value it may be in itself, is of special importance here as an introduction to, and, after that, as an aid for, the better appraisement of the events narrated in the next chapter.

CHAPTER III

REMOVAL PROJECT

As time passed, both the Baptist Education Society of the State of New York and the Hamilton Literary and Theological Institution maintained by it took on more and more of a state-wide denominational character. In consequence, when the charter for Madison University was obtained in 1846, about one-fifth only of the trustees named in it were Baptists who resided in Hamilton, whereas approximately four-fifths of the whole number were denominational leaders in other parts of the state, especially in Albany and in New York City and its environs, while one was the pastor of the First Baptist Church of Rochester. This one was Rev. Pharcellus Church, who was a graduate of the Hamilton Literary and Theological Institution and the recipient in August, 1847, of the first honorary degree of D.D. conferred by Madison University. The fact that Madison University was generally deemed to belong to the whole denomination in the state, and thus to be the subject of denominational responsibility for its welfare, had greatly to do with the removal project.

REMOVAL PROJECT

The financial problem relative to the maintenance of the Institution at Hamilton was always present and pressing. It grew as fast as the Institution, or faster. Some contributions toward the support of the Institution were voluntarily made, but most of them had to be solicited either by personal visitation or through letters and printed communications.

Eventually it became necessary to employ Baptist ministers as agents to make a business of systematically visiting the churches and selected individuals of the denomination in quest of funds. When an agent visited a church, he usually preached a sermon that enlisted the sympathies of the congregation in the work of the Baptist Education Society, for which a special collection was then taken. Incidental to his mission of gathering funds, an agent was expected also, as he went here and there, to keep a lookout for desirable young men for the ministry and to endeavor to get them to go to Hamilton for their needed educational training. His salary or commission and traveling expenses might take 25 or 30 per cent of his total collections.

The seriousness of the financial situation which developed was shown in the report dated October 9, 1849, of "The Trustees of Madison University to the Baptists of the State of New York, in Conven-

ROCHESTER AND COLGATE

tion Assembled" (at Albany). The trustees who made the report, referring to the conditions when they assumed office after the incorporation of the University, said:

"Our most urgent difficulty was connected with the want of funds. We were entirely destitute of those endowments which all experience had shown to be necessary to the successful prosecution of such objects. . . . . Accordingly, at our very first meeting, in June, 1846, we commenced our efforts to endow the University. Everything depended on enlisting the right agents. Committees were appointed for this purpose, and correspondence on the subject was had with leading brethren in various parts of the state. The results were discouraging. No agent could be induced to take hold of the enterprise, and difficulties developed themselves which seemed to forbid all hope of success for an indefinite time to come. . . . . And in September, 1847, at a conference of our board with that of the Education Society, on receiving the peremptory declinature of the last agent we appointed, it was the unanimous conviction of the members present that for the present all hope of endowment must be abandoned; and we adjourned without making any new appointment, or other provision for prosecuting the effort.

REMOVAL PROJECT

"It was at this period of darkness and anxiety that the measure of removal suggested itself to the minds of some of our members, and was by them laid before others. It was as a means of extricating our beloved University from the embarrassments which surrounded it, and of opening before it a career of success and usefulness in a more favorable position, that this measure was first suggested, or that it was ever regarded with favor."

The removal proposed was of Madison University to the city of Rochester. The immediate approval with which the project was looked upon by the Baptists of Rochester and vicinity, as promising both great denominational and local benefit, and how soon and energetically they took active steps to promote it, are indicated by the meeting that they held on September 12, 1847, or five days after the question of the removal was said to have been introduced into Rochester. The record that was kept of that meeting—"a meeting of the friends of Madison University, called Sept. 12th, 1847, at the First Baptist Church in Rochester"—showed that Rev. W. Metcalf, of Brockport, presided, and that Dr. Henry W. Dean, who was the clerk of the First Baptist Church and a prominent physician in Rochester, acted as secretary. Of the transactions of the meeting, the record said:

ROCHESTER AND COLGATE

"At the request of the chairman, Dr. [Pharcellus] Church stated the object of the meeting to be the consideration of removing Madison University from its present to some more eligible location in western New York. In the course of his remarks, Dr. Church alluded to some of the inconveniences of the present location of the Institution: its distance from the main thoroughfares of the state; also, to its heavy pecuniary embarrassment." He thought "its removal to a more accessible and populous place, the erection of new buildings, etc., might awaken an interest favorable to the Institution, to the denomination it represents, and to Christianity universally"; thought "Rochester, from its relative position in western New York, with its many and growing facilities, an eligible location for such an Institution."

John N. Wilder, of Albany, who, like Dr. Church, was one of the incorporators and trustees of Madison University, said, among various other things, that he thought "the present location out of the way and in other respects unfavorable"; and thought, "all things considered, Rochester to be a good location for the University, which would meet the wishes of the majority of the denomination in the state." A little later he said: "We do not wish to remove it, unless it can be partially

REMOVAL PROJECT

endowed, after good location and buildings are provided."

"In order to get an expression of the meeting," Dr. Church introduced a resolution, which was "carried unanimously," "that it be regarded the sense of this meeting that Madison University be removed to Rochester."

E. Pancost, of Rochester; Rev. H. Stanwood, of Rush; and a Mr. Spear, of Palmyra, were mentioned as other participants in the meeting.

A committee "to confer with the Baptist churches in western New York, in reference to this matter," was appointed. It consisted of Dr. P. Church, of Rochester; Rev. H. K. Stimson, of Wheatland; Rev. W. Metcalf, of Brockport; Rev. Mr. Bainbridge and Rev. Mr. Herington, of Livingston County; E. Huntington and E. Boardman, of Rochester.

On September 20 an adjourned meeting was held at the First Baptist Church in Rochester. William H. Cheney, who established the first furnace and foundry in the city, presided. John N. Wilder presented a resolution, which was adopted as the sense of the meeting, to the effect that, before making the outlays required to put in good repair the buildings occupied by Madison University and to erect a new building that was needed,

ROCHESTER AND COLGATE

and before attempting to raise the partial endowment which the University ought to have, "we recommend to its Board of Trustees to apply to the legislature for its removal to the city of Rochester, or its immediate vicinity." He gave a number of reasons why he thought that ought to be done.

Other resolutions, consonant with that one, were introduced by Dr. Church, G. W. Burbank, E. Huntington, D. R. Barton, A. G. Smith, and, a second one, by Mr. Wilder; all of which were adopted. Mr. Burbank's resolution was:

"That the Baptists of Rochester and Monroe County are able to raise thirty thousand dollars for the purpose of removing Madison University; and that immediate measures be taken to secure from them that amount."

The next meeting "to consult in relation to the interests and prospects of Madison University, and to take measures to secure its removal to western New York," was held in Greece, on October 5 and 6. Thence adjournment was taken to meet in the vestry of the First Baptist Church in Rochester, on October 13.

At this meeting in Rochester, John N. Wilder "reported progress of the subscription list, and read letters from various persons urging us by all means to go forward in the accomplishment of the re-

REMOVAL PROJECT

moval of Madison University to Rochester." Rev. Z. Case, of Ogden; E. Harmon, of Wheatland; and Rev. H. Stanwood, of Rush, who were appointed a committee on resolutions, reported the following, which was passed unanimously:

"*Resolved*, as the sense of this meeting, That the time has arrived when it is the duty of the friends of education to take measures for the removal of Madison University to Rochester, or its immediate vicinity, and that we feel it to be a duty we owe to the cause of Christ, the interests of our denomination in the state, and to the cause and interests of education generally, to use and employ our influence and our pecuniary means to accomplish this object."

The first subscriptions toward the endowment of Madison University, if removed to Rochester, were made by John N. Wilder and members of the First and Second Baptist churches of Rochester. Then a meeting was held in the Baptist Church at Wheatland, on October 18, at which there was started a raising of subscriptions that in less than three weeks amounted to $5,800. That meeting was addressed by Rev. H. K. Stimson, pastor of the church, by John N. Wilder, and by "Messrs. [Oren] Sage, Huntington, and Rev. Pharcellus Church, of Rochester."

ROCHESTER AND COLGATE

Another important event was the sending out through the state of about a thousand copies of a printed letter dated Rochester, October 22, 1847, and signed by David R. Barton, William N. Sage, Elon Huntington, Henry W. Dean, Alvah Strong, *Committee.* The letter read, in part:

"We beg your attention to the subject of the .... removal of Madison University from its present, to some location in western New York, where, we think, the interests of our denomination, and of education generally, may be better subserved.

"We believe the individuals who instigated this movement have been, and are, the substantial friends of that venerated Institution, and simply desire to extend its influence.

"It is now twenty-seven years since the Hamilton Institution .... went into effective operation. .... How mighty the change which has since taken place. .... This vast current of events acting upon our educational interests .... has brought on a crisis which seems to render a change in the seat of our operations both desirable and inevitable to their success. ....

"But if Madison University is removed, where shall it go? Eastern and central New York are filled with colleges and universities, while western New York, with a population of nearly six hundred

REMOVAL PROJECT

thousand inhabitants, is without a college, except . . . . at Geneva; and therefore . . . . would . . . . lift it into the prominence which it must attain before it will realize the just expectations of its friends. This could not fail to be the result, if placed in an eligible position, on a liberal and unsectarian basis, and adapted to the wants of the public. Should it be placed at Rochester, ... easy of access by means of its railroads, canals and lake navigation, it would enjoy every advantage for obtaining students and of extending its means of usefulness. . . . ."

This letter, with some changes in its phraseology and considerable insertions of new matter, was also given some newspaper circulation, under the heading: "To the Friends of Madison University (Circular)."

In its revised form it began:

"DEAR SIR: We address you on a subject of the deepest moment—that of transferring Madison University to this city, and making this the future seat of our educational operations, as a denomination, for this state. This movement does not originate with us, but from the opposite extreme of the state—or rather, it is forced upon us by the altered state of things since the origin of the Hamilton Institution."

ROCHESTER AND COLGATE

Near its close, the letter said:

"The other denominations have come to our assistance with a noble zeal and a praiseworthy liberality. They have merged their interests in the enterprise, under the sense of a common necessity for a university in western New York."

That there was some plan on foot for the removal of Madison University to a new site was first discovered and heralded by the newspapers in the latter part of October, 1847; and thereafter it received considerable attention from certain portions of both the secular and the religious press.

One of the first papers to mention it was the *Syracuse Journal*, which said that it understood that it was proposed to remove the University to a point more central and easy of access, and that the two places named for its future location were Syracuse and Rochester. "Already," the *Journal* continued, "has Rochester, with her characteristic appropriating propensity, commenced operations to secure its removal to that place. The Baptist denomination in Monroe County [in which Rochester is situated] is large and wealthy, perhaps more potent in its influence than in any other county in the state, except New York. It will require but little effort to bring all this influence to bear in favor of locating it in Rochester, notwith-

REMOVAL PROJECT

standing it will be so far west as to be a source of expense and inconvenience to the eastern and southern sections of the state. . . . . The general preference is strongly in favor of this place [Syracuse]. We have only to employ ordinary agencies and we shall secure its location in our midst, increasing our business and dispensing its blessings to generations yet to come."

That article was quoted by both the *Rochester Daily Democrat* and the *Rochester Daily American*, of October 26. In both papers it was followed by comments, especially about the "fling" at Rochester. What the *Democrat* had to say was written by John N. Wilder, who frequently used his pen, as well as often his voice, in behalf of this University project. In the *American*, Alexander Mann, a Baptist, who was then the editor of that paper, said, among other things: "Now that this subject has been brought to the notice of our citizens by the journals of other places, we trust they will give it the consideration it deserves. . . . . Much has been said within the past year concerning the establishment of a university in Rochester. The time, may we not hope, is now come to accomplish what all desire. And should it be deemed advisable to remove the Madison University hither, we have no hesitation in saying that it will be heartily and

ROCHESTER AND COLGATE

liberally welcomed by the citizens of all denominations as a priceless blessing to the community."

Two days later, the *American* said: "We desire to bring this subject distinctly before the minds of our citizens. The establishment of a new college here has recently been much discussed. But the removal of one already well grown, and furnished with faculty, students, libraries, and apparatus, would be vastly more desirable. We should have from the beginning a large and strong institution, which a new one could hardly be."

On October 28, the *Syracuse Journal* published a communication, probably written by Rev. R. R. Raymond, pastor of the First Baptist Church of that place, saying:

"A similar effort was made by the Buffalonians, some years ago, by the offer of an endowment of $100,000, but without success. In the estimation of the friends of the Institution, the time had not yet arrived to make such a change expedient. The present movement originates in Rochester, and has already proceeded so far as to afford good promise of a successful issue; particularly as the opinion generally prevalent among the influential friends of the University seems to favor *some* change in its location. The Rochesterians . . . . appear to have been thoroughly roused to the object, and to have

REMOVAL PROJECT

so far compassed it as to be on the point of dispatching an efficient committee to the eastern congregations to consummate the subscription."

On that same day (October 28), there were distributed in Rochester about two hundred printed invitations "to attend a meeting at the City Hall, this (Thursday) evening, to hear some statements relative to the removal of Madison University to this city, and to take part in a discussion in reference to that object." This was signed by William Pitkin, F. Whittlesey, Washington Gibbons, N. E. Paine, Everard Peck, H. E. Rochester, Elias Pond, F. W. Holland, H. Stilwell, Alexander Mann, Darius Perrin, Samuel D. Porter, Joseph Putnam, Henry Cook, L. Ward Smith, W. W. Ely, E. Peshine Smith, Isaac Butts, H. L. Winants, S. Hamilton, W. H. Perkins, E. Shepard, "and others."

The speakers at the meeting were Dr. Pharcellus Church, John N. Wilder, Isaac Hills, Ebenezer Griffin, J. W. Dwinelle, Dr. Chester Dewey, Rev. Samuel Luckey, Rev. F. W. Holland, I. F. Mack, Thomas Kempshall, D. R. Barton, "and others," a report of the meeting said.

A resolution favoring the removal project was passed unanimously. Besides, the following were appointed a committee "to obtain subscriptions and to take measures for further prosecuting the great enterprise of supplying the demand of a university for the people of western New York": Dr. Chester Dewey, William Pitkin, Rev. F. W. Holland, A. J. Brackett, Dr. Pharcellus Church, N. E. Paine, Rev. J. B. Shaw, Oren Sage, E. Huntington, and D. R. Barton.

That public meeting, the *Daily American* of November 2 said, "was largely attended by influential gentlemen of different religious denominations. The utmost friendship for the project was manifested on all sides, and a determination expressed to carry it forward to completion." The men who signed the call for that meeting, and those who addressed it, were also men of several different religious denominations, some of them being prominent ministers, while others were leading business men of the city.

On November 1, the *Rochester Daily Democrat* said: "The friends and supporters of Madison University propose, with the consent of the legislature, to remove it to some favored locality on the great central avenue through the state. Many of them have fixed on Rochester as the most eligible, and as the Rochester University [the one incorporated in 1846] has failed of endowment, they design to make this the university for western New York."

REMOVAL PROJECT

Again, the same paper said, on November 4, in an article written by Mr. Wilder, "Madison University is to be removed. . . . . Buffalo once offered it a home, and a hearty welcome, but Buffalo is too far west. New York and Albany, in days gone by, have each intimated their desire to adopt it; but the cities on the North River are too far east. Utica, Syracuse, and Rochester are now making the most energetic efforts to secure it. . . . . Which place shall have it?"

In an article published on November 9, Mr. Wilder stated: "The friends of the University of Western New York, who took the initiative some months since to establish a literary institution here, cordially unite in the movement [for the removal of Madison University to Rochester], and many of them have transferred their subscriptions to the books of Madison University."

Meanwhile, the *Utica Gazette* said that it understood that an intention to remove Madison University was very seriously entertained and would probably be carried into effect within a very short time. "Utica possesses every requisite sought for in the new location, and in many respects presents superior inducements over any other place. We learn, moreover, from the best authority that it has been much talked of, and if the favorable disposition toward it is met on the part of its citizens with as much zeal as has been manifested in other places the probabilities are altogether in favor of its being the place selected."

About the middle of November, the *Auburn Daily Advertiser*, referring to the subject of the removal of Madison University, asked: "Why not make an effort to secure removal to Auburn? .... Will Auburn, which offers more advantages than any town yet named, permit the prize to slip from her without an effort?"

On the question of the future location of Madison University, the *Buffalo Courier*, of November 5, said:

"For several reasons we prefer that it shall be removed to Rochester. The principal of these are: That there is no institution of the kind in western New York. It is farther from other colleges, and will there occupy a vacant field—one in which it is highly desirable that such an institution should be located. It is upon the great thoroughfares of the state, and thus the University would be brought out into the world. The citizens of Rochester are enlightened and liberal in their educational views, and the Institution would there find spirits congenial to its high ends and purposes, and energy and enterprise to sustain it and enlarge and extend

REMOVAL PROJECT

its usefulness. It is in the midst of one of the most substantial agricultural regions of the country, which would furnish to it a large number of students. The principal reason, however, for preferring Rochester to Utica or Syracuse, is the first. . . . . There appears to be a general feeling in the East—in New York and Albany, and in the southern part of the state, in favor of Rochester."

The *New York Recorder* (Baptist) said, on November 27, in the course of a lengthy editorial:

"Rochester, Syracuse, Utica, have each called for the University, and each place has set forth its peculiar claims. Hamilton, likewise . . . . has claims . . . . and we regret that Hamilton has not spoken, if she has anything to say. . . . . The general feeling sets strongly towards removal, and we presume the thing will be done. Indeed many of the best friends of the University regard the question of removal as one of life or death. . . . .

"The first question, in considering the matter of removal, relates, as it seems to us, to the advantages of a more populous and wealthy location—a city on a great thoroughfare, rather than a retired though healthy and beautiful village. . . . . We do not say—we do not believe—that a great Babel like New York is the best place to acquire an education; but we do say, other things being equal, that

ROCHESTER AND COLGATE

a city like Rochester, Syracuse, or Utica, is to be preferred to a place of great quiet and seclusion. The world—men and things as they are—form the material on which the student is to work; let him see the world—men and things as they are—as well as books. . . . . From the tenor of these remarks it is plain enough that our opinions are in favor of a removal of Madison University . . . . provided the necessary endowment is furnished. . . . .

"But, between the cities named, which, all things considered, is the best location? . . . . Would it not be best that Madison University should be planted *in the centre of unappropriated territory?* Western New York has already a population of more than half a million, with no large, well-endowed, efficient and liberal university. Planted there, on a liberal basis, furnishing the amplest facilities for an education of the highest stamp, administered with a courteous, unsectarian bearing toward all sects and parties, Madison University would remove all necessity for another university, and no other would be originated. It would seem as if divine Providence has left that center open for her approach. Madison University is invited to become the University of Western New York—her seat Rochester."

In Buffalo, on November 30, a meeting was

REMOVAL PROJECT

held at the Washington Street Baptist Church, to consider the subject of the endowment and removal to Rochester of Madison University. The meeting was addressed by Rev. Levi Tucker, pastor of the church, who was a graduate of the Hamilton Literary and Theological Institution, and by Dr. Pharcellus Church, Deacon Oren Sage, and John N. Wilder. It was afterward reported that "all seemed to feel the importance of doing something for the aid of the University; and there was expressed but one feeling in relation to the desirableness of its removal to western New York." Furthermore, within a couple of days subscriptions amounting to about $5,000 toward the endowment of the University, in the event of its being removed to Rochester, were obtained from members of the church and congregation.

But within little more than a week after the *Recorder* had expressed its regret that Hamilton had not spoken with regard to her claims concerning the University, her silence was very disconcertingly broken. On December 6, 1847, an adjourned meeting of citizens of the village was held at the Baptist Church, "for the purpose of hearing the report of a committee previously appointed to express their sentiments on the subject of the contemplated removal of Madison University to Rochester." The report was about four thousand words in length. After its adoption, "3,000 copies of it were ordered to be printed and circulated without delay." It was styled *A Candid Appeal*, with the qualifying statement, *Of the Citizens of Hamilton to the Friends and Patrons of Madison University throughout the State of New York*. It was addressed to "Fellow Citizens," and took up, as the first question, "Ought Madison University to be removed from its present location?" After arguing that to a negative conclusion, it proceeded with a consideration—in a favorable light for Hamilton—of such subjects as the size, location, accessibility, rural surroundings, healthfulness, and citizenry of Hamilton, and the cheapness of living there, together with the advantages of a rural village over a populous city as the location for a college or a university. It also advanced reasons why it would be disadvantageous to remove the University to Rochester. It went further, and asserted that the University could not be legally removed from Hamilton, and that "so deeply are our vital interests concerned in the decision of this question of removal, you could not expect us to yield our rights before pressing the case to the utmost extreme of litigation. . . . . We should feel called upon by a solemn sense of duty

REMOVAL PROJECT

to vindicate our rights with whatever ability, energy and perseverance we may possess."

Although this Candid Appeal purported to be the production of a committee, its real authorship would appear to be indicated by its being referred to in the "Madisonian Annals" by Professor Spear, as "Dr. Eaton's Candid Appeal."

Some effects of the Candid Appeal were apparently shown in the somewhat conservative attitude of "a meeting of friends of Madison University residing in New York, Brooklyn, and vicinity," that was held on December 29, 1847, in the First Baptist Church of New York City, "to consider the propriety of the removal of the University to some more western location in the state, and the question of an endowment." Palmer Townsend, of Brooklyn, presided. Rev. A. Wheelock was appointed secretary. John N. Wilder explained what had been done in the western part of the state, and the reasons therefor. That was followed by a discussion in which a number of persons joined. Dr. William R. Williams, pastor of the Amity Street Baptist Church, New York, offered four resolutions, which were:

"That this meeting deems Madison University to require and to deserve from its friends throughout the state a large endowment of not less

ROCHESTER AND COLGATE

than $150,000, the subscriptions being payable, however, on their attaining the sum of $100,000.

"That a site, within the bounds of the state, further towards the west than its present location, promises an increase of its strength and usefulness, could the removal be honorably and harmoniously effected.

"That if, by uniting the measure of such removal and that of endowment, the latter may be greatly facilitated, and if the more western churches secure their share, properly a large one, in such endowment, a proposition then presented by such western churches for the removal of the University would deserve the very respectful consideration of the boards, both of the Education Society and of the University.

"That, should the friends of the Institution in the western regions of the state contribute the sum of $75,000, it would, in the judgment of this meeting, be the duty of the friends of Madison University in other portions of the state to complete by their prompt and liberal subscriptions the residue of the requisite endowment."

These resolutions were referred to a committee consisting of William Colgate, Dr. Williams, and Rev. J. L. Hodge (of Brooklyn), to report on them at a later date.

REMOVAL PROJECT

The correspondent in New York City of the *Baptist Register* wrote to it, after this meeting:

"The subject of removing the Institution is here regarded as a very grave and important one, demanding great caution. Judging from the remarks made at the meeting, all here are disposed to do that which will be most likely to promote the interests of the University. Not a doubt is entertained but that the agitation of the subject will most seriously affect the future prospects of the Institution. Should it be removed, the friends in and near Hamilton may be seriously affected, and . . . . should it remain, the friends in western New York may feel themselves called upon to concentrate all their energies in establishing an institution demanded by local considerations. Under these circumstances, the friends here are regarding the crisis with very deep solicitude."

The committee to which Dr. Williams' resolutions were referred rendered its report at an adjourned meeting held on January 6, 1848. The report said that the question presented was virtually twofold: Should the Seminary [Madison University] be endowed? Should it be removed?

"Some, looking to its past history, would, perhaps, prefer that it should continue dependent on yearly appeals to the churches. They think it more

ROCHESTER AND COLGATE

likely to be preserved, thus, pure and spiritual in its character; and they deem, also, that course better suited to the resources of our churches, which would give, as these friends suppose, cheerfully and easily as annual contributions, sums far surpassing the interest of any principal which they could or would bestow, in bulk, as an endowment. They dread, also, endowments for religious uses, as inviting cupidity and treachery, and as often affording to heresies a vigorous and permanent stock, whereon these baleful grafts of error may fix and thrive, whilst without such aid, these parasitical plants would often perish from the want of native zeal and of inherent vitality."

However, the conclusion that was reached on this branch of the inquiry was that, in the judgment of most of the friends of the Institution who had examined the subject, the Institution must, as a college, to keep abreast of kindred and rival institutions, receive an endowment which, to be of any practical value, must be liberal as well as secure.

With regard to removal, the report was more non-committal, expressing a need of further reflection and fuller developments of divine Providence. At the same time it gave warning that,

"If the Rochester subscription should, on the

REMOVAL PROJECT

removal being refused, become the germ of a new and rival institution, cutting off the western patronage of Madison University, this would prove a grave, and a wasteful, if not a ruinous, schism."

The *New York Recorder*, in referring to this report, said that it was not intended to express any decided opinion on the question of removal. "Friends of the University in this section are entirely uninfluenced by sectional feeling. Rochester and Hamilton are all one to them, so far as local considerations are concerned."

Nevertheless, when Dr. Williams individually renewed his offer of the four resolutions, which it had been agreed that he might do, they were evidently unanimously adopted.

Again, the *Candid Appeal* was apparently largely responsible for a mass meeting, or "Convention of Ministers and Laymen," being held in the village of Wyoming, on January 11, 1848, and the issuance therefrom of a somewhat lengthy *Address to the Baptist Churches of the State of New York, on the Subject of Removing and Endowing the Madison University*. Indeed, it has been asserted that this *Address* was intended to be an answer to the *Candid Appeal*; and that it was written by Dr. Church. Still, the *Address*, which it was enjoined that no Baptist should leave unread, was signed by a committee of sixteen that was composed of the following ministers: Jesse Elliot and Gibbon Williams, Wyoming; P. Church, Rochester; H. Daniels, Le Roy; H. K. Stimson, Wheatland; J. L. Richmond, Warsaw; H. B. Ewell, Pavilion; O. D. Taylor, Moscow; Henry Smith, Pike; and these laymen: J. R. Doolittle, Warsaw; David Burbank, Deacon P. Capwell, and Deacon D. Howard, Wyoming; General Rawson Harmon, Jr., General Theron Brown, and Elisha Harmon, Wheatland. Jesse Elliot, chairman, and William N. Sage, secretary, certified that the *Address* was unanimously adopted and ordered to be published. Portions of it were as follows:

"DEAR BRETHREN: The object of our meeting is to deliberate and pray over our educational interests, and to inquire whether our only University and Theological Seminary in this state may not be relieved from its embarrassments and placed in a condition of greater usefulness by being removed to this section of the state and endowed up to $100,000 besides buildings and grounds. . . . .

"We see no hope of any considerable increase from tuition under the present circumstances of the University. But transferred to a great, destitute field, more extensive and more populous than the one where it now is can ever be, how is it possible

REMOVAL PROJECT

that it should fail both of giving more education and of realizing greater consequent income?

"We all feel that it is undesirable to multiply our colleges. We already have more than are well supported. As Baptists and friends of Madison University, also we feel reluctant to establish one in our section of the state, lest it should turn away students and money from *that*. . . . .

"Taking all these things into account, we honestly believe that, in removing the University from central New York, we are inflicting no serious injury in that quarter, because *one* [Hamilton College, at Clinton, about eighteen miles northeast of the village of Hamilton] is as much as they need, while by this step we are supplying a pressing and deeply deplored necessity in the western division of the state. . . . .

"We cannot mistake our duty to the country in which we live, which is the only great division of the state destitute of a university. As a denomination, we have refrained from acting in this section of the state, for fear of inflicting injury upon our interests at Hamilton. But we have now come to the deliberate conviction that central New York may resign to this portion of the state one of its colleges with equal advantage both to the one that *comes* and to the one that *remains*. Is it not preposterous that two such institutions should exist within eighteen miles of each other? . . . .

"We wish you to understand, brethren, that we did not move in this thing till we had taken advice from some of the principal men on both boards. We corresponded with the faculty on the subject, who felt that their position did not render it fitting and proper for them to take an active part in the movement, though they were free to confess their conviction that some radical measure of the kind was necessary to relieve the Institution of its embarrassments and to realize from it the utmost possible good to the cause of Christ and to the interests of a suffering world. We sought advice from distinguished brethren from Chicago to Boston, all of whom gave us unequivocal proofs of their interest, provided it would result in an endowment, and the most of them urged it with the utmost zeal.

"Dr. Wayland . . . . wrote us, at an early period, that for a long time he had heard nothing that gave him so much pleasure as this movement; . . . . he strongly urged the vigorous prosecution of the enterprise. He says, 'Go forward, and let nothing deter you, except the indication that it is not the will of God.' We do not give his exact words, his letter not being present, but we give its spirit.

"Thus from east to west, from north to south,

REMOVAL PROJECT

we were cheered onward in our work until we had arrived at a certainty of accomplishing it. . . . . Meantime a counter-movement began to manifest itself at Hamilton. . . . . We name these things, not to complain of any one, but as indicating the danger to which our dearest interests are exposed, and the liability of our being deceived by specious appearances.

"Shall we, as a denomination in the great state of New York, longer keep our only University in the disgraceful condition of begging its living from door to door? There is no hope of relief where it is. Six years of fruitless endeavor for an endowment has proved this. . . . .

"Why, our beloved brother, J. N. Wilder, ... stands at the head and front of this [movement]. . . . . It was his fortune to pass a few weeks last summer in Hamilton, where he became familiar with the state of things at the seat of our educational operations, ... and was fully impressed with the conviction . . . . that they never can be relieved in their present location. Impelled by these impressions, he has since left his home, his business, and at his own expense, without fee or reward, has given up his whole time to do what he believed was indispensable to the relief and enlargement of our University."

Strong and widespread, however, as was the demand for the removal of Madison University to western New York, and in particular to Rochester, the opposition interposed to it was very determined, as the *Candid Appeal* declared that it would be. Consequently, when application was made to the legislature for authority to remove the University, it was met with strenuous objection. The main arguments for both sides were briefly summarized in the report made to the Assembly on March 9, 1848, by the committee on colleges, academies, and common schools, concerning the bill "In relation to the Madison University." This report is preserved as Document No. 111, in Volume III of *Assembly Documents* of 1848. It says:

"That a large majority of the trustees of the University desire the passage of the bill, and express the opinion that without it the Institution will cease not only to prosper, but probably to exist. That the University being without endowment is dependent upon the charity of the Baptist denomination, under whose auspices it was established; and that the annual calls on the churches are met with increasing impatience, and must soon be unattended with success.

"The trustees who have appeared before the committee declare that it is very improbable that

REMOVAL PROJECT

the University will ever be sufficiently endowed at Hamilton; that the friends of its removal to Rochester have already subscribed $75,000 for that purpose, and promise to increase their subscription to the sum of $100,000; and that Syracuse will contribute nearly an equal amount, if it should be located in that city.

"It was also urged that the University, if located in western New York, on the main route of travel and in a large and flourishing city, would be much more likely to prosper than in central New York, in the vicinity of rival colleges and in a village difficult of access and containing a small population.

"The citizens of Hamilton and their friends, on the other hand, claim that the highly flourishing condition of the University is of itself sufficient evidence of the excellence of its location—in the valley of the Chenango, one of the most lovely and healthful in the state—in a village celebrated for the morality and intelligence of its inhabitants, and free from the vices and temptations usually attendant on a large city.

"They also insist that the New York and Erie Railroad and other works, contemplated or in progress, will shortly render Hamilton one of the most desirable places in the state for the seat of a

ROCHESTER AND COLGATE

large literary institution, and that if sufficient time be allowed, the University will be liberally endowed in its present location.

"Many other considerations were presented, which it is unnecessary to notice, as the committee are happily freed from the necessity of expressing an opinion on the propriety of the passage of the bill referred to them, the parties interested having agreed upon a compromise bill, which it gives the committee much pleasure to report and recommend to the favorable consideration of the House."

On April 3, 1848, the legislature passed "An act in relation to the Madison University," as a compromise measure. It was as follows:

"SECTION 1. The trustees of the Madison University are hereby authorized to change the location of the said University, from the village of Hamilton to the city of Syracuse or the city of Rochester or the city of Utica; provided they shall within one year from the passage of this act, file with the secretary of state a resolution of their board, adopted by a majority of the votes of all the members constituting said board, electing to make such change, and determining at which of said places said University shall be located.

"SEC. 2. In case the residents of the village of Hamilton shall on or before the second Tuesday of

REMOVAL PROJECT

August next raise the sum of fifty thousand dollars in cash or satisfactory security, and pay the same to the president of the said Board of Trustees for the purpose of a permanent endowment of the said University, or shall deliver to said president a bond to the said trustees, with a satisfactory security, to be approved by said president, in the penalty of one hundred thousand dollars, with a condition to pay within one year from the passage of this act, to the said trustees, the said sum of fifty thousand dollars for the purpose of such endowment, then nothing in the first section of this act contained shall be deemed to authorize the removal of said University, but the same shall remain where it now is."

How nearly the conditions of Section 2 were complied with was a subject of dispute. The prevailing view of the Board of Trustees of the University was shown by the passage, on the night of August 14, 1848, of two resolutions, which opponents of removal alleged were in these words:

"*Resolved* (the board of the Education Society concurring), That it is expedient to remove the Madison University to the city of Rochester, or its vicinity. The said removal to be conditioned that legal difficulties interposed be found insufficient; and that Seneca B. Burchard, Ira Harris, and

Robert Kelly be a committee to examine such difficulties, and hear arguments. Upon their favorable report such removal to be unconditional.

"*Resolved*, That whenever such satisfactory report shall be received, and the removal made unconditional, the officers of the board be authorized to file, according to the provisions of the statute, the following resolution in the office of the secretary of state: '*Resolved*, That the Madison University do hereby elect, pursuant to the authority given them, to remove to the city of Rochester, or its vicinity.'"

On or about January 26, 1849, a resolution of election to remove the Madison University to Rochester was filed with the secretary of state. That was immediately met with a suit in which a temporary injunction was obtained against proceeding with the removal.

Then, on February 16, there was filed a "Memorial," which, as "No. 37," occupies thirteen pages of Volume II of *Senate Documents* of 1849. The "Memorial" asked for the repeal of the act in relation to the Madison University passed on April 3, 1848, authorizing the removal of the University under certain contingencies. The "Memorial" was countered by a "Remonstrance" against such repeal, which was filed on March 3, 1849, and, as "No. 52," fills

REMOVAL PROJECT

seventeen pages of said volume of *Senate Documents*. Volume II of the *Journal of the Assembly* for 1849 records (p. 836) the presentation, on March 14, of a petition for a repeal of the law allowing the removal of Madison University, and (p. 873) the bringing in, on March 15, of a bill entitled "An act to provide for retaining the Madison University in the village of Hamilton." However, that bill was not enacted into a law; nor was the law authorizing the removal of the University repealed.

Afterward, the advocates of removal had the annual meeting for 1849 of the Baptist Education Society called to be held on Tuesday, June 12, at Albany, as neutral ground, instead of at Hamilton, in August, as had been the previous custom. It was also arranged that meetings of the two boards— that of the Education Society and that of Madison University—should be held at the same time and place as that annual meeting. But the meeting of the society could not be held as intended, on account of the following notice, which was found in the *Albany Evening Journal* of Saturday, June 9:

"Baptist Education Society of the State of New York. Supreme Court. In the matter of the application of Benjamin W. Babcock, Henry G. Beardsley, and Theodore Burchard, to set aside the election [of 1848] of trustees of the Baptist Educa-

ROCHESTER AND COLGATE

tion Society of the State of New York, and for a new election of trustees for said society, and for other relief:—

"Pursuant to an order of the Supreme Court, held at the town of Rome, in the county of Oneida, this 7th day of June, 1849, in this case, Notice is hereby given that by virtue of said order the meeting of the Baptist Education Society of the State of New York, called for the 12th day of June, instant, at the city of Albany, has been postponed until the further order of the Supreme Court upon the motion now pending and undecided in the above-mentioned proceeding. By order of the Court."

This notice was given too late to prevent the assembling at Albany of a considerable number of representative Baptists from different parts of the state. As members of the society, they adjourned the meeting thereof without transacting any business; but, immediately after that, as so many individuals, they organized themselves into an Educational Convention, and deliberated on the educational problems that confronted them denominationally in the state.

There were two resolutions that were presented by John N. Wilder, and adopted by the convention. They were:

REMOVAL PROJECT

"That our convictions are decided that Madison University should be removed to Rochester."

"That this convention recommend to the Board of Trustees to commence their next term in the city of Rochester, should the injunction now resting upon it be removed."

Another resolution that was adopted was one offered by Dr. William R. Williams. It was:

"That, while showing no indifference to legal rights, yet desiring to cultivate fraternal union, this convention recommends the appointment of a committee of ten for the purpose of maturing, if possible, some scheme of compromise, which may end litigation, and restore, as far as may be, union and co-operation among our brethren; and this meeting suggests as an outline of such scheme, that it should save the property at Hamilton and the subscriptions at Rochester—plant the University at Rochester, and preserve a literary and theological school, at least one of shorter course, at Hamilton."

The following persons were appointed on such committee: Rev. S. H. Cone, D.D.; Rev. W. R. Williams, D.D.; Rev. A. Bennett; William Colgate, Esq.; Hon. Friend Humphrey; Hon. Henry Tower; William Cobb, Esq.; William Sage, Esq.; Palmer Townsend, Esq.; and Roswell S. Burrows, Esq.

ROCHESTER AND COLGATE

The suits pending against Madison University and the Baptist Education Society were decided in August, 1849. In the case attacking the validity of the election in 1848 of trustees of the Education Society, the election was set aside, and a new one ordered. But there was a dismissal of the case or cases in which the removal of Madison University and the property and operations of the Education Society had been enjoined, it being held that the plaintiffs, who were not parties to the contract for the location of the Seminary at Hamilton, did not have such an interest that they could maintain a suit for an injunction against the threatened removal.

A new suit was then begun, with Daniel Hascall, the only survivor of the original parties to that contract, as one of the plaintiffs. The decision which Justice Philo Gridley subsequently rendered in this case was what was practically finally determinative of the movement for the removal of Madison University to Rochester. The title of the case was *Daniel Hascall and Medad Rogers* vs. *The Madison University and the Baptist Education Society of the State of New York.*

In this case, Justice W. F. Allen, on August 28, 1849, granted the plaintiffs an injunction restraining Madison University, its trustees, officers, and

REMOVAL PROJECT

agents, from removing its site from Hamilton, and from using the funds of the Baptist Education Society otherwise than pursuant to the contract between the two corporations; also restraining the Baptist Education Society from removing its Literary and Theological Seminary from Hamilton, and from using its funds otherwise than pursuant to the purposes of the founders and donors of said Institution. A motion was thereafter made for the vacation or modification of the injunction in relation to Madison University, no question being raised on that application concerning the right of the plaintiffs to insist upon the continuance of the Theological Seminary at Hamilton. The motion was heard by Justice Gridley. He rendered a decision at "Oneida Special Term, March, 1850," which is reported in Volume VIII of *Barbour's Supreme Court Reports*, on pages 174–89, denying the motion on the state of facts presented by the pleadings and the affidavits that were read on the motion.

One of the contentions of the plaintiffs was that the condition of the act of 1848, on which the right to remove the University was made to depend, was never performed. In proof of this they referred to the resolutions passed on the night of August 14, 1848, heretofore quoted, and especially

ROCHESTER AND COLGATE

to the words, "or its vicinity," following "city of Rochester." If the resolution contained the clause, "or its vicinity," most clearly the condition of the act, Justice Gridley held, was not complied with. The vicinity of Rochester might mean a location within a mile beyond the limits of the city, or in any of the neighboring towns. Without undertaking to say what might be the balance of evidence when all the testimony should be taken, on the papers before him on this motion he was brought to the conclusion (in the absence of all explanation) that the resolution had been shorn of the fatal words subsequent to its passage by the board.

Another question raised was whether the committee referred to in the resolution had ever performed the duty assigned to them in such a manner as to confer on the officers of the board the power to file the resolution for removal; for, if they had never so performed it, the act of filing the resolution was unauthorized and void. This, like that other question, had to be decided on the papers in the case, and, based on them, the decision was that the committee had not so discharged the trust delegated to them as to authorize the filing of the resolution of removal, "even admitting that a trust of this kind were capable of being delegated at all."

REMOVAL PROJECT

Having come to the conclusion that Mr. Hascall had the right to restrain the trustees of both corporations from the prosecution of an enterprise which, if carried out, would be fatal to the interests of the Seminary at Hamilton, Justice Gridley added: "I desire, for the purpose of preventing any misconstruction, to say, that I by no means intend to impute a design to any of the parties to commit a wrongful or injurious act. They have, doubtless, acted in entire good faith. I speak only of the legal character of certain acts which have become wrongful, because not warranted by law."

The injunction in this case was made permanent by a decree entered by Justice Gridley on or about April 23, 1850, at Morrisville.

Various explanations have been given as to why, where, and how the project for the removal of Madison University to Rochester originated. Some of them have already been mentioned.

The prompt and vigorous action taken at Rochester to bring about the suggested removal led to the statement sometimes being made that the idea of removal had its origin in Rochester, or "at the west," which, in this connection at that time, meant the same thing.

On the other hand, Dr. George W. Eaton, of Madison University, said, in the "Historical Dis-

ROCHESTER AND COLGATE

course" delivered on August 5, 1869, which was published in *The First Half Century of Madison University:*

"The origin was *local* and *personal*. The idea was born in a storm of personal indignation raised by an act of the Education Board in adjusting the new relations between it and the Board of the University. The act related to the distinguished professor of biblical theology [Dr. John S. Maginnis]. .... The wrong, however great it might have been, was rectified by rescinding the act or vote. .... *Here* at *Hamilton* and *then*, in that *tempest* of feeling, did the thought of removal come into being. .... We never supposed that the people of Rochester had anything whatever to do with the origination of the removal enterprise."

Professor P. B. Spear's "Madisonian Annals," in that same volume, supply these dates of the year 1847:

"Sept. 1st, The special meeting of the two boards; difficulties affecting the chair of theology are *settled;* the University Board comes into management of the 'Hamilton Literary and Theological Institution.'

"Sept. 7th, The question of 'The Removal' introduced into Rochester from Hamilton."

In a speech which Senator Thomas H. Bond, of

REMOVAL PROJECT

Oswego, delivered on March 28, 1849, in the Senate at Albany, he said:

"The 'Remonstrance' says, 'The suggestion of removal was first made at the west.' The Rochester gentlemen in their first circular on the subject say: 'This movement does not originate with us, but from the opposite extreme of the state.' The fact is, both are mistaken, and those who understand the origin and cause of the removal project smile at all the elaborate *after-thoughts* to account for the extraordinary phenomenon.

"How and by whom, then, did the project originate? In order to answer this question, I must lift the veil, and expose some of the secret springs through whose instrumentality this engine was put in motion.

"In the adjustment of the relations between the two boards, subsequently to the procurement of the University charter, it was deemed proper to re-elect the several professors. It so happened, however, that when the two boards met for the election of their respective officers (and each board elected its own), one of the old theological professors, Mr. Maginnis, having become unpopular, from some cause which it is unnecessary to mention, was superseded. This transaction engendered a good deal of ill-feeling in the bosoms of many who were his

ROCHESTER AND COLGATE

friends; so much so that both boards were immediately called together, and he was unanimously reinstated.

"Here is the source of this removal project. Up to this period, not a word had been uttered; not a syllable had been published in regard to this matter. Professors, citizens, all, had been calm and quiet as the seven sleepers.

"As soon as this event happened, however, to which I have alluded, John N. Wilder, Esq., who was then temporarily residing in the village of Hamilton, in company with his friend, Mr. Maginnis, visited the city of Rochester (the latter gentleman was on his way to the West), and while there 'the happy discovery was made that an important section of western New York was just as much in want of a college as Madison University was of an endowment.' Soon after their return to the village of Hamilton, this ball of removal was put in motion, and it has been rolling onward from that day to this."

Again, when the removal plan was nearing defeat, the *Democratic Reflector*, of Hamilton, scented a "plot" to withdraw the faculty and students from Hamilton to Rochester, and then divert the patronage into the latter channel; and it charged that Dr. Maginnis was "the person who incautiously developed it."

REMOVAL PROJECT

Sprague's *Annals of the Baptist Pulpit* said that Dr. Maginnis was "keenly sensitive to injury, and did not hesitate to make it manifest by appropriate demonstrations. But it was little more than a flash of feeling; and when it was over the kindly spirit at once resumed its accustomed control. . . . . He was among those on whom the labor and responsibility of the removal very largely rested."

From these and other bits of evidence, it may not be far amiss to conjecture that Dr. Maginnis may have been the author of the suggestion which was made in September, 1847, for the removal of Madison University (for its own welfare) to Rochester.

However, be these things as they may, this suggestion of removal was new only in the effect which it had. In an article published in the Rochester *Daily Democrat* of December 11, 1846 (when efforts were being made to raise funds for the University of Rochester that was chartered that year), Dr. Pharcellus Church said:

"I had hoped at one time that the Episcopalians might transfer Geneva College to this city, or that the Methodists would locate a college here, and it has actually been a subject of conversation and inquiry whether the Baptists throughout the state would not concentrate their resources upon the establishment of a university in Rochester. .... But, as for myself, I would prefer a college for Rochester that should be non-sectarian and adjusted to the mass of the people in western New York, rather than to have my own denomination locate here their educational operations. .... The Baptists expended nearly ten thousand dollars a few years ago to found one at Brockport, but suspended operations for the time being on account of the great failures of 1837."

After he had resigned his pastorate of thirteen years in Rochester, in order to accept a call to a church in Boston, Dr. Church, on July 15, 1848, wrote to the *Baptist Register:*

"As I am soon to leave the state, it is due to history that I should give a brief statement of the *causes* which set in motion this removal enterprise. .... It so happens, in the providence of God, that I have been active in this enterprise almost from its inception, and can therefore speak of its *causes* from personal knowledge.

"Twelve years ago the subject of removing the Institution from Hamilton to Buffalo was much talked of; and several years after, I am told, an essay was written in Hamilton itself, by an owner of real estate, showing that the proper seat of the University is *Rochester*. Whatever may be said of

REMOVAL PROJECT

the impracticability of these facts, they still show that there were considerations operating upon men's minds to make them feel that the Institution was suffering from the disadvantages of location, and that removal was the only remedy. . . . .

"Other influences more specific came to our aid, among which was the interest which some of us had long felt to see western New York supplied with the means of liberal education. . . . . We have always put the two together, the relief of Madison University and the supply of western New York. We aimed at accomplishing the first by means of the second, as *supply* and *demand* are always mutual helps to each other. . . . .

"We could not be indifferent to the wants of this section of the state. I had myself been long excogitating a plan for establishing a university here. A charter for one was at length obtained [that of 1846], from which I stood aloof, partly because I did not like some of its features, and partly because I feared I should turn funds from Madison University, and thus increase its embarrassments. Still, in April, 1847, I was officially notified of the following vote: 'At a regular meeting of the Board of Trustees of the University of Rochester [the one incorporated in 1846], held on the 21st inst., you were unanimously elected a

ROCHESTER AND COLGATE

trustee in the place of Henry Dwight, resigned.' Consequently, between this and the 1st of September, when our effort for removal began, I was in great doubt whether to accept of this appointment or not. . . . . My mind had been for months deeply interested in two separate and distinct objects, an endowment for Hamilton, and a university for western New York, prior to my embarking in the removal enterprise. . . . .

"Our plan was to accomplish both objects under one, if possible; and, if not possible, then to look out by other modes for a university for western New York, doing in the meantime as well as we could for Hamilton. We think that the future growth of Madison University imperiously requires its identity with western New York; that here it can help itself as it never can be helped at Hamilton."

Alvah Strong said, in his *Autobiography*, which he wrote about 1880:

"In the decade opening with 1840, there was a growing conviction among the friends of our denomination in this state that Hamilton was not the best place to develop most effectively our great educational work as a denomination. It was the conviction of our best minds that new life and more thorough work would be inspired in min-

REMOVAL PROJECT

isterial education by removing the schools to another locality. The discussion continued to go on and was kept up from year to year, until the question culminated, and the leading members of the Hamilton [Madison] University resolved that if Rochester would make an earnest effort, with a tangible inducement, the schools should be moved to this place; or, failing in the transfer, the faculty would resign their offices at Hamilton and unitedly come on to, and found, an entirely new institution in Rochester."

Viewed in the light of three-quarters of a century after the removal of Madison University to Rochester was sought, it seems very fortunate that the plan was not successful. Because it failed, there are now two large, strong, and growing Universities where otherwise there would probably be only one of them. Moreover, the two are both being more and more needed as the years go by, which most, if not all, of the men who advocated removal then believed could never be possible.

At the same time, it is very likely that considerable good resulted from the movement for removal, both to Madison University and toward providing a university for Rochester and western New York.

But for the interests that the plan awakened and united, it is hardly conceivable that a univer-

ROCHESTER AND COLGATE

sity would have been established in Rochester under the auspices that one was in 1850, if at all. The general regard of the Baptists for the Institution at Hamilton, and their belief that they could not sustain two colleges or universities in the state, would have deterred them from attempting to found a second one.

Nor was the effort to remove Madison University to Rochester without decided benefit to that University. It aroused a local interest and raised up elsewhere friends for the University, whereby the latter was soon relieved of its immediate distress and was subsequently liberally developed, as it might not otherwise have been.

"Madisonensis" (who was presumably Professor John H. Raymond), writing to the *New York Recorder*, at a comparatively early date in the course of the controversy, said:

"The western movement, whether well or ill advised, sprang up among the friends of the University, and was prosecuted, beyond all question, from the most honorable motives—not to injure Hamilton, but to benefit the Institution; not to promote any private or selfish end, ... but really at no little personal inconvenience and pecuniary cost, with the hope of securing a great public good. . . . .

REMOVAL PROJECT

"Finally, when both boards were convened at a special meeting in September last [1847], to reconsider an act of the Education Board, it was distinctly and generally understood by the members present that the feelings of brethren in other sections of the state were such that the attempt to obtain an endowment was utterly hopeless, and had better for the present be abandoned. The door of hope now seemed effectually closed; and many who had toiled and waited long were on the point of giving up in despair.

"It was at this darkest hour in the history of our beloved Institution that another of those marked interpositions of divine Providence occurred, which have so signally illustrated its course from the beginning. A sudden light sprang up in the west. Without an agency, and without any expectation of the kind on the part of either of the boards or the faculty, a spontaneous movement was originated there, having its source in the *popular demand* for a western college, and promising to make requisite provision without even the expense or trouble of asking for it. We have called this an interposition of divine Providence. We believe it to have been so. Whether the design be to stir up the friends of the present location to liberal action, or to make that provision *elsewhere* which cannot

ROCHESTER AND COLGATE

be made *there*, time must develop. In either case, it is to the University 'life from the dead.' "

The new life that Madison University subsequently took on is indicated in the report, dated January 31, 1852, which the trustees of the University made for the academic year ending in August, 1851, to the Regents of the University of the State of New York. The trustees said:

"Though the [Madison] University has suffered embarrassments by the attempted removal, yet since the question was settled, the trustees have had the satisfaction of seeing a strong *upward* tendency pervading all its affairs. Their effort to create a partial endowment and their new appointments in the Faculty of Instruction have proved alike successful and happy. The number of students is rapidly increasing, the public patronage is growing, and the divine favor is manifested in a variety of forms."

Now, for the founding of the University of Rochester!

CHAPTER IV
UNIVERSITY OF ROCHESTER

The higher educational needs of the city of Rochester, of western New York, and to an extent of the Baptist denomination, which were sought to be supplied by the removal of Madison University to Rochester, remained as great as ever after the plan for such removal had been abandoned. But so strongly had they impressed themselves on the minds of the leaders of the removal project that these men felt it to be their duty to continue their efforts to meet those needs. This they determined to accomplish through the establishment of a new university at Rochester, at whatever cost of further labor and self-sacrifice it might require; and it did require much of both, as well as of zeal and perseverance. Some of the men were actuated principally by the advantage they thought it would be to one or another of the interests that would be subserved, though most of the men had at heart the serving of all the interests that might be expected to be benefited by the founding of the University of Rochester.

It was at Albany that the new plan was adopted.

ROCHESTER AND COLGATE

A committee that had been appointed by the Educational Convention that was formed there and held on June 12 and 13, 1849, and by it empowered to call a state convention of the Baptists, issued a call, which the Board of Trustees of Madison University seconded in an address to the denomination, and in which friends of Hamilton also united, for an Educational Convention which was held in Albany on October 9 and 10, 1849. This convention was one of the largest that the Baptists of the state had ever held up to that time. The attendance was nearly six hundred, and from all sections of the state; as notable, too, for the character of the men who composed it as for their number.

The first resolution offered at this convention was:

"That in the opinion of this convention the necessities of the Baptist denomination in this state render it alike expedient and a duty to establish a university at Rochester with collegiate and theological departments, unless some compromise shall be effected with the friends of Hamilton for the harmonious and united support of a collegiate institution at Rochester, and a theological one at Hamilton."

This resolution was presented by Rev. Alonzo

UNIVERSITY OF ROCHESTER

Wheelock, of Vienna, Ontario County, who previously had been the pastor of the Sixteenth Street Baptist Church in New York City. It was deliberately discussed, adopted, and followed by the introduction, by Rev. Isaac Westcott, of another resolution, which was also adopted, namely:

"That a committee be appointed to report to this convention a plan for organizing a university at Rochester in accordance with the resolution just adopted."

This committee was composed of Isaac Westcott, W. R. Williams, A. M. Beebe, Henry Davis, E. E. L. Taylor, J. S. Backus, and Marsena Stone.

The committee, in the hope of bringing about a compromise, began its report:

"Your committee would express the opinion that the interests of the denomination, of religion, and of literature, might be best advanced by the consent, on the part of Hamilton, to relinquish the University charter for the use of an institution to be exclusively *collegiate* at Rochester; and that, in such an event, and, after such modification of the constitution of the Education Society as shall preserve to Baptists the control of Baptist theological instruction, the churches throughout the state should reunite and rally around Hamilton as the single seat of theological education."

ROCHESTER AND COLGATE

For use in case this arrangement could not be effected, the committee then proceeded to give the following "outlines" of a plan for organization at Rochester, recommending that the details should be left for future consideration:

"The collegiate and theological institutions to be distinct in organization and government; but the same individual may be eligible to a chair in both faculties.

"The collegiate organization, in case Madison University be not transferred thither, shall include a board, in the organization of which the control shall be reserved perpetually to the Baptist denomination; and the Committee of Nine hereinafter named shall be empowered to nominate members for such college board.

"That the *earliest* attention be given to the collegiate institution.

"That a Committee of Nine be appointed to draft in detail a plan of the proposed collegiate and theological institutions, and that they report such plan to a meeting which said Committee of Nine are empowered to call; and that R. G. Burrows, R. Kelly, J. N. Wilder, Ira Harris, Henry Davis, V. R. Hotchkiss, Henry Tower, J. S. Backus and R. R. Raymond become such Committee of Nine."

The first paragraph of the report, after being

carefully considered, was adopted. Then this resolution, which was introduced by Sewall S. Cutting, D.D., the editor of the *New York Recorder*, was passed:

"That this convention recommends, as the terms of an amicable adjustment of all our educational difficulties, that the University charter be surrendered to Rochester by the friends of Hamilton, and that the project for a Theological Department be abandoned by the friends of Rochester; and that the denomination give their united support to both Institutions—to the one for collegiate education, and to the other for theological, on the former basis of the Hamilton Literary and Theological Institution."

Thereafter the remainder of the report and the report as a whole were adopted. In addition, a committee of five, of which Henry Tower was chairman, was appointed to confer with the plaintiffs in the suit pending against Madison University, with a view to inducing them to discontinue the suit and abandon all further legal controversy.

This plan for a compromise was looked upon very hopefully by almost everyone. For example, the *Baptist Register*, which was friendly to Hamilton, said editorially, on October 18:

"This numerous and highly intelligent body of

ROCHESTER AND COLGATE

brethren, collected from various parts of the state, brought their deliberations to a delightful and harmonious close. . . . .

"The proposition to place the Institution at Hamilton on its former footing previous to the granting of the University charter, and to make it the great and only Theological Seminary of the Baptist denomination in the Empire State, and the establishment of an exclusively literary college at Rochester, under the Madison University charter, ... developed the plan which could be greeted, and was greeted by all. There was, however, this proviso: Should the transfer of the charter be refused, or the injunction be retained, then a college, with a theological department, to be established and endowed at Rochester. The preliminary provision being entirely satisfactory to all, it received a cordial and unanimous greeting, and the alternative in case of non-compliance being so entirely unsupposable, there was hardly room left for a doubt of its full and complete consummation."

Still the plan for a compromise and all efforts of the committee appointed to make it effective failed; the chairman of the committee announcing, November 12, "that the citizens and brethren at Hamilton cannot at present feel it to be for their interest to accept the compromise."

UNIVERSITY OF ROCHESTER

This brought into activity the Committee of Nine appointed at Albany in October. It met at Rochester on December 6, 1849, and proceeded to draft a plan for a new university, to be named "The University of Rochester." The Committee provided that the University should be governed by twenty-four trustees, and designated the persons to be made the first trustees. It then appointed a committee, consisting of Ira Harris, William L. Marcy, Friend Humphrey, George R. Davis, and John N. Wilder, to confer with the Regents of the University of the State of New York, and to take all necessary means for obtaining a charter for the new University. Another committee that it appointed consisted of Oren Sage, John N. Wilder, Elon Huntington, G. W. Burbank, David R. Barton, William H. Cheney, and Albert G. Smith, to take charge of the business of obtaining subscriptions for the University, and to employ such agents as they might deem expedient. This committee, however, was subsequently superseded by one appointed by the trustees, which was headed by John N. Wilder and of which D. R. Barton was one of the members.

The qualifications for admission into any of the undergraduate classes of the University, the Committee of Nine said, should be fully equal to those

ROCHESTER AND COLGATE

then required for admission into the corresponding classes in Madison University, while the course of studies to be pursued should be equal to that of any of the colleges in the state.

On January 31, 1850, the Regents of the University of the State of New York issued a written instrument, which was then and has since commonly been termed a "provisional charter," as it was in fact. It, however, purported to be only an approval of the place where, plan on which, and funds with which, it was intended to found and provide for an institution to be known by the name of the University of Rochester, with approval also of the persons proposed for the first trustees. Two years' time was allowed for completing the plan and getting and investing funds as proposed, though the time was afterward extended.

This instrument stated that the petition which had been presented "prayed for the grant of a provisional charter, for the establishment of an institution of the highest order for scientific and classical purposes. . . . . The system of education to be pursued in the said institution 'to extend to all the branches of science and learning, which are taught in the most approved universities of this country, including not only those studies of conceded importance, wherever the benefits of true scholarship and learning are admitted, but also those which are more especially applicable to the institutions of our own country, and the wants of the present time.'"

The Institution, according to further statements made with regard to it, was to be located at or near the city of Rochester, in the county of Monroe, and the corporation thereof was to be known by the name of the University of Rochester.

The funds with which it was proposed to endow this Institution were, in the first place, the purchase of a suitable lot for the site of the proposed University, and the erection of suitable buildings thereon, to be reasonably worth in all $30,000, and the investment of at least $100,000 in bonds and mortgages for the institution of professorships and the general support of the college.

The superintendence of the interests of the Institution and the power to confer degrees were to be committed to a board of twenty-four trustees, the following persons being proposed as the first trustees: William L. Marcy, Friend Humphrey, Ira Harris, John N. Wilder, and Smith Sheldon, of Albany; Frederick Whittlesey, William Pitkin, Everard Peck, Elon Huntington, William N. Sage, David R. Barton, Edwin Pancost, and Elijah F. Smith, of Rochester; Robert Kelly and William R.

ROCHESTER AND COLGATE

Williams, of New York; Robert R. Raymond, of Syracuse; Henry Tower, of Waterville, Oneida County; Seneca B. Burchard, of Hamilton, Madison County; John Munro, of Elbridge, Onondaga County; Alonzo Wheelock, of Vienna, Ontario County; James Edmonds [Edmunds], of Yates, Orleans County; R. S. Burrows, of Albion, Orleans County; Ransom [Rawson] Harmon, Jr., of Wheatland, Monroe County; and [V. R.] Hotchkiss, of Buffalo.

On May 11, 1850, an Educational Convention of the Baptists of the state was held in Rochester, pursuant to a call of the Committee of Nine. A report of the Committee was presented, which stated the plan that it had prepared for a university, and what it had done or caused to be done, as well as gave a plan for a separate theological institution. Thereupon the convention passed resolutions to the effect that, "We cordially approve the steps taken by the committee to procure a charter for the University of Rochester." "We will accept the charter by the earliest practicable fulfillment of all the conditions which it prescribes." "We recommend to the trustees of the University of Rochester to take immediate measures to fill the department of instruction, and to open the University at the earliest practicable period."

UNIVERSITY OF ROCHESTER

At the afternoon session of the convention a society was formed, called "The New York Baptist Union for Ministerial Education," which, it was provided, "shall sustain a theological school." That school, when founded, was named the Rochester Theological Seminary.

The *New York Recorder's* report said:

"The convention was held in pursuance of the plan laid down by the Albany convention. It met for the purpose of giving full effect to the proceedings of the Committee of Nine appointed at Albany to arrange the details of a university project, with provisions for theological education adjoined. This work the convention most happily performed. . . . .

"Rochester is . . . . precisely the spot for a university. It has the requisite social advantages without the dissipating luxuries of the great marts of commerce. It has a sober and religious population—a population which will both appreciate a good university and take proper care of it. We are glad that the University is to wear the name of the city. We believe the liberal interest manifested by the citizens in its establishment a pledge that it will abide in their hearts and share their prosperity.

"Then what a region for a university is western New York! What a blessing that divine Providence left it open for occupation at such a juncture!

ROCHESTER AND COLGATE

As long as man is to find food in the products of the soil, so long will western New York invite an industrious and thriving population. . . . . Inhabited now by a working and virtuous population, the region will remain so peopled if the institutions of education and religion are well established and perpetuated. All that region is interested in this enterprise. This University comes with a blessing to every man's door. Its influence will be felt . . . . in every department of life, in every vocation, and at every home. The project attempted is not a work for one generation, but for children's children."

The *Watchman and Reflector*, of Boston, said that this meeting was more than usually spirited, harmonious, and determined; that things had assumed aspects more promising than could have been anticipated by the most sanguine friends of removal; that there seemed to be a united feeling among the great body of the churches to sustain institutions, both of ministerial and collegiate education, in this beautiful and most promising location.

Thus had the prospects for the founding of the University of Rochester become very encouraging. Still, the raising of the funds needed for equipment and endowment was scarcely half accomplished.

UNIVERSITY OF ROCHESTER

Some subscribers under the removal plan declined to transfer their subscriptions to be used for a new university, while others increased, or even doubled, their original subscriptions, in order to aid in the establishment of the University of Rochester. There was in behalf of either plan no lack of effort to get subscriptions. President Augustus H. Strong, of the Rochester Theological Seminary, said, in the *Historical Discourse* which he delivered in 1900, "Our cities and villages were canvassed for subscriptions as they never had been before and as they never have been since. . . . . Let us remember that this was at a time when our people had not a tenth of their present means. The result can only be regarded as a wonderful example of enlightened and conscientious liberality."

Dr. Strong's father, Alvah Strong, stated, in his *Autobiography:* "I myself went out with Messrs. Wilder, [Oren] Sage, Edmunds, and others, from store to store and from house to house, in city and country, soliciting subscriptions to the University."

When the limit of what could be accomplished in this manner, that is, by volunteer workers at their own expense and at no little self-sacrifice besides, had been virtually reached, leaving much yet to be done, special agents were employed for the

ROCHESTER AND COLGATE

work. Thus it came about that announcement was made, under date of June 20, 1850:

"Brethren Edmonds [Edmunds], Westcott, Freeman, and Galusha, take the field this week, as agents for the University of Rochester. . . . . They are all well known as brethren beloved, and as having been long and honorably identified with our educational interests in this state. Brethren Freeman and Edmonds have been the main pillars on which the Institution at Hamilton has rested. They have nursed its finances, gathered its students, and of late years for whatever of funds or favor it has received from the denomination it is largely indebted to them. . . . . All these brethren have in times past been the advocates of Hamilton, and would as soon speak reproachfully of their own youth as of its past history. . . . ."

This is quoted from the second number of the *Annunciator*, a four-page paper of which at least five numbers were issued in 1850–51, "Devoted to the Interests of General and Ministerial Education," and intended primarily to make friends and to aid in getting subscriptions for the University of Rochester. In the first number (dated April 4, 1850) it was stated that the paper was issued by the committee that the Committee of Nine had appointed to procure subscriptions. Yet it would

UNIVERSITY OF ROCHESTER

seem that its publication was largely, or entirely, a matter of private enterprise, more or less under the management of William N. Sage, for it was said, in a "Notice," that communications should be addressed to him, and that "the expenses attending this effort bear so heavily upon a few that we are compelled to ask that all letters should be post-paid." There is also good reason to believe that Mr. Wilder had considerable to do with the publication.

Commenting on the "Rochester Subscription," the first number of the *Annunciator* said:

"The citizens of Rochester have shown a noble liberality in their subscriptions to the endowment of the University which bears the name of their city. While conceding the necessity of its having a denominational character and control, and expressing frankly their preference for an institution controlled by those whose religious opinions correspond with their own, they have given their names for sums really munificent, asking only that a strong religious influence may pervade the Institution. They have stipulated nothing; they have exacted nothing. It has been freely and fully stated what the character of the University will be, both in its board of instruction and in its board of control; all have subscribed with a clear understanding on these points."

ROCHESTER AND COLGATE

Under the heading of "Monroe County," it was declared: "We think we can say with truth that the wealth, intelligence, influence, and piety are largely represented on the subscription for endowing the University of Rochester."

Again, the *Annunciator* stated:

"The *quality* of the University of Rochester seems to be much more an object of solicitude than does its denominational character. A very large proportion of those who have subscribed thus far have done so with the expectation of educating their sons within its walls. They say: 'Whatever you give us, let it be good.'" "Sober-minded men express it as their belief that there will always be in the University from one hundred to one hundred and fifty students from Rochester and its immediate vicinity."

With regard to what was intended to be the character of the University, the *Annunciator* declared, on different dates, that the University of Rochester would be consecrated to the great principle of *soul liberty;* that it was not local in design— was not restricted in its plans by sectional lines. It said further:

"No one can fail to see that a university, offering to all alike who desire them the advantages of general culture, and a seminary having in view the

UNIVERSITY OF ROCHESTER

theological training of candidates for the gospel ministry .... must of necessity be differently organized and conducted. The former should, quite manifestly, be open to all who wish to realize the benefit of a good education, irrespective of their religious opinions, or the profession or pursuit for which they are preparing. . . . .

"A *religious spirit* should doubtless pervade every institution of learning, to whatever class it belongs; while it is found to be a point of practical wisdom to have, besides, the endowment, organization, and control, of at least such as belong to the grade of colleges and universities, mainly in the hands of some denomination of Christians. In this sense they may be, and should be, denominational; in this sense the University of Rochester is so. To expect more than this is to require the introduction of what is not only foreign to the design of such institutions, but will be sure to operate directly in opposition to the design, and what is, moreover, inconsistent with the provisions of any charter which the laws of this state will allow. . . . .

"The Baptists of New York will surely not think less of their University because it proposes to do good in various ways, and, while offering the advantages of literary culture to their candidates for the sacred office, dispenses the same benefits so widely that many others may realize them."

"Our undertaking is a magnificent one. We propose, ... as a denomination, ... to establish at a great central point the machinery for thorough ministerial and general education. We propose to be a blessing to our children, to our churches, to our state."

On May 13, 1850, or two days after the Rochester convention, a number of the trustees of the University held an informally called meeting in the committee room of the First Baptist Church. A "committee of seven on the plan of instruction to be pursued in the University" was appointed. It was composed of Robert Kelly, William R. Williams, F. Whittlesey, Chester Dewey, Thomas J. Conant, A. C. Kendrick, and J. H. Raymond.

At that meeting, too, a resolution was passed to the effect that the New York Baptist Union for Ministerial Education should have the privilege of forty scholarships for students to pursue the undergraduate course in the University, without charge for tuition. This was to be so if in the aggregate $40,000 should be subscribed for the endowment of the University by persons who should request that their subscriptions might be appropriated for such scholarships. The resolution also provided that

UNIVERSITY OF ROCHESTER

subscribers contributing $1,000 for the purpose of educating gratuitously for the Christian ministry in said course should each, his heirs and assigns, enjoy the privilege of one scholarship in perpetuity. This resolution was evidently intended to carry out similar provisions made by the Committee of Nine and approved by the Rochester Convention, as aids to the collegiate education of young men for the ministry and toward raising the endowment required for the University. However, it was not until July 7, 1857, that the Board of Trustees of the University could say that it accepted the list of subscriptions presented as fulfilling the conditions upon which the forty scholarships for free tuition were granted to said Union.

What was designated the "first duly called and notified regular meeting of the trustees" was held on September 16, 1850, in the committee room of the First Baptist Church. The organization of the board under what was termed the provisional charter was perfected by the election of John N. Wilder, president; F. Whittlesey, vice-president; William N. Sage, secretary; and Edwin Pancost, treasurer.

To have the immediate superintendence of the University, the trustees created what they denominated the Executive Board of the University of

ROCHESTER AND COLGATE

Rochester, to constitute which board nine trustees were chosen by ballot. They were: John N. Wilder, R. S. Burrows, E. F. Smith, Edwin Pancost, E. Huntington, D. R. Barton, Everard Peck, F. Whittlesey, and William N. Sage. The Executive Board made Mr. Wilder its chairman, and Mr. Sage its secretary.

Toward a faculty, the trustees selected Asahel C. Kendrick, D.D. (a nephew of Dr. Nathaniel Kendrick), professor of the Greek language and literature; John F. Richardson, A.M., professor of the Latin language and literature; John H. Raymond, A.M., professor of history and *belles lettres;* and Chester Dewey, M.D., D.D., LL.D., professor of the natural sciences. The salary of each was fixed at $1,200 a year, payable quarterly. The first three were scholars of prominence who had been for years professors in Madison University. Dr. Dewey was a distinguished veteran educator who resided in Rochester. He was a Congregationalist, but the others were Baptists.

For a limited service, to give instruction in Hebrew or some other department of study, at a compensation of $300 a year, the Executive Board was authorized to engage Rev. Thomas J. Conant, who was to be one of the professors in the Rochester Theological Seminary.

UNIVERSITY OF ROCHESTER

The Executive Board was especially directed to hire for three years, at $800 a year, what was known as the United States Hotel Building, and to make such repairs on it as were necessary to adapt it to the use of the University. The property was then practically vacant.

Furthermore, on September 16 the committee which was appointed on May 13 presented its *Report to the Board of Trustees of the University of Rochester, on the Plan of Instruction to Be Pursued in the Collegiate Department.* The report was approved. It contained about 15,000 words, and, when printed, made a pamphlet of 50 pages. The latter part of the title indicated that it was expected that the University of Rochester would become a university in fact, as well as in name.

The arrangement of what might be deemed the best curriculum for a college, one that might be expected to meet the demands of the times, was not altogether an easy matter. There was a great deal of criticism, even by men of education, of the general course of study in the colleges, which, moreover, did not attract sufficient numbers of students. With variations as to the relative amount of attention given to different subjects in different institutions, the ordinary course of study, which was substantially the same for all students and occupied four years, the committee said, gave the first place to Latin and Greek. Mathematical science was rated next in importance. History, *belles lettres*, moral and intellectual philosophy, and political economy might be grouped together as another class of studies embraced in the course. Natural philosophy, chemistry, and occasionally some other of the natural sciences, as geology, botany, or mineralogy, usually had a limited time allotted to them.

Not only did the committee have no desire to disparage classical studies in any measure, but it declared that its members were unanimously of the opinion that the critical and extended study of Latin and Greek was of the greatest value for those who aimed at distinguished scholarship and who would devote the requisite time to their education. Nevertheless, it was realized that there were men whose views carried weight, who maintained that the study of those languages was of less benefit to the majority of young men than were some other branches of study. Besides, the committee itself believed that a course of useful and sound education could be arranged without Latin and Greek. But the committee strongly deprecated crowding too many studies into the regular course, advising rather the taking of an additional year of study.

UNIVERSITY OF ROCHESTER

In brief, the committee, after considering the merits and the defects of the established collegiate system, was led to the conclusion that it was, on the whole, admirably adapted for intellectual training and, in its main characteristics, should not be abandoned. The feature of a systematic course of instruction especially should be maintained, in order to secure even development and a fair amount of general culture. But the existing range of studies was too restricted to meet the educational wants of the people. The means of instruction in many very useful and important branches was not provided.

The subject of providing study rooms and boarding halls also demanded notice, in the opinion of the committee, which proceeded to say:

"The trustees will probably determine, without a dissenting voice, to make no provision of the kind. It will certainly simplify the whole management and government of the Institution. The character of the community of Rochester justifies the belief that the experiment of boarding students in families may be made with safety and without difficulty. All that will be necessary is that the parents or guardians of the young men should take proper care in selecting places for them. The trustees and officers of the University may also properly exercise some supervision over each case and cause to be applied the moral restraints that may from time to time be necessary. With these precautions, the intimacy of the young men in families is calculated to throw safeguards about the morals, to enlarge the general tone of thought, and to exercise a refining effect upon the manners. The silent influence of the social virtues is an important element in the formation of character. These are influences which students, at their impressionable period of life, peculiarly need, and which are not found in the habits that prevail in halls and commons."

The plan of instruction proposed was very much like the elective one which Dr. Francis Wayland introduced at Brown University. It was also quite similar to one with which experiment was being made at the Free Academy (now the College) of the City of New York, which institution Robert Kelly had helped to organize.

Moreover, the position taken by the committee with reference to dormitories was in harmony with advice given by Dr. Wayland. According to the *Memoir* by his sons, he wrote to Mr. Wilder: "What I want you to think of is, first of all, not to erect dormitory buildings for students. It leads to half, or more than half, of the trouble in colleges, and besides absorbs money that might be much better employed. If you start on this principle, it will save you from much expenditure."

The "Plan of Instruction" was the subject of a long editorial in the *New York Recorder* of October 23, 1850, of which paper Martin B. Anderson became the editor on June 12, 1850. He said in that editorial:

"We have read this document with great interest and pleasure—the more so as it is understood to be from the pen of a merchant, Robert Kelly, Esq., of this city, the chairman of the very able committee to whom the subject was referred by the trustees. . . . .

"While, if it were our duty to assist in any way in carrying the proposed plan into effect, there are some details that we might wish to modify, we must express our most hearty concurrence with the general tone of the reasonings, statements, and recommendations of the report. . . . . It defends with ability the results of past experience, while it yields to all the reasonable demands of progress, and manifests a disposition to give a fair trial to the views of those who wish to provide instruction in colleges adapted to the special wants of business men. . . . .

"The advantages of the plan are that it secures the benefit of two regular compulsory courses that are to be studied in classes. The elective studies are so selected and come so late in the course that they prevent the student from availing himself of the privilege to avoid the more difficult branches, while by it he is saved the evil of having his mind confused by studying too many subjects in a short time. . . . .

"A true *man* is a nobler thing than a doctor, or a lawyer, or a merchant. Let us then shape our educational systems to make *men*, and then upon this foundation we can superimpose the special learning that will adapt them to any of the special pursuits of life. We would not, however, be understood as wishing the same means of development to be applied to all. Let the right principles underlie a system, and we would not be bigoted in our attachment to the course of study which we individually prefer. . . . .

"We are glad, then, to see a movement which will meet the wishes of those whose pursuits in life are to be active, rather than literary or professional. . . . . But we believe there are some serious mistakes which are often made by those who contend for what they call practical education. . . . . We cannot separate ancient from modern learning, and whatever course of education presupposes the possiblity of so doing must be inadequate and

UNIVERSITY OF ROCHESTER

partial. . . . . Far distant be the time when a mechanical and money-making age shall banish profound science and generous learning from the schools where minds are to be trained to act upon and form the future of our Republic and of the church of Christ. . . . . The college, like the church should *lead* rather than *follow* the public mind.

"But we must close with one word on the proposal to abolish the dormitory system. We think that in this the report is right. In those colleges which have buildings already erected, or which are situated in places where accommodations are not readily obtained in private houses, the present system will continue. But where a new institution is to be started, we think that the opinion of the great majority of teachers would be that of the committee. . . . ."

Something of the application which was made of the "Plan of Instruction" is indicated by the following excerpts from the first (1850–51) catalogue of the University of Rochester:

"The plan of instruction is so adjusted as to allow any, who choose, to omit the study of Latin and Greek, either throughout the course, or, with the advice of the faculty, after the completion of the Sophomore year, substituting in their stead modern languages and a more extended mathematical and scientific course. Hence the students in each class will be divided into two sections corresponding to the two courses of study, and distinguished as the *classical* and *scientific* sections.

"The regular course for all students extends through four years, at the end of which time those who pass a good examination in the prescribed studies are admitted to a degree, those who have pursued the entire classical course, to the degree of Bachelor of Arts, and those who have pursued the entire scientific course, to that of Bachelor of Sciences.

"Young gentlemen desirous to attend the recitations of particular departments are allowed to do so, provided they have the requisite preparation for the studies of those departments."

"The plan of the University," as the trustees stated in their first report to the Regents of the University of the State of New York, "dispenses with college dormitories as a source of many serious evils, and supposes the discipline of intelligent, moral, and religious families among which the students find homes to be in every way more desirable."

Nevertheless, a large part of the first building occupied by the University—the old United States Hotel Building—was used by the University as a

UNIVERSITY OF ROCHESTER

dormitory for students. That the Executive Board lost no time in getting possession of that building is shown by the record of a meeting having been held "at the University buildings" on October 10. It was then voted "to paint the front part of the building dark; make a plank platform in front of the building; repair railing and fix locks, bolts and doors; purchase 100 common wood chairs, 5 pine tables, 6 arm chairs, 7 box stoves, 7 boxes for wood, 30 settees for chapel." "A desk for chapel was presented by F. Whittlesey."

The building was constructed of brick and stone, in 1826, at a cost of about $25,000. It was L-shaped and four stories high. It had a frontage of 100 feet on Buffalo Street (now Main Street West), being on the north side of that street, a little east of Elizabeth Street. The wing which extended back from the west end of the main part of the building was also of considerable length and capacity. The building was used first for hotel purposes, and afterward, at one time and another, it was, as a whole or in part, used for a manual training school, for two different schools for girls, and for a railroad station.

The whole building, according to one account, contained a convenient chapel, two halls for the two literary societies, fourteen well-lighted and

ROCHESTER AND COLGATE

well-finished rooms, convenient in all respects for recitation, lecture, library, and reading-rooms; and sixty-five smaller rooms, affording accommodations for the same number of students. In connection with the building, it was further said, there were grounds sufficiently spacious for the comfort and convenience of the members of the University.

The *Annunciator* of January 1, 1851, in describing the building, said: "Under the whole is a large basement used for cellars, and a refectory for such students as choose to board with the janitor. The rooms of the literary societies are on the lower floor of the main building, and are being tastefully decorated and conveniently and elegantly furnished. Adjoining these rooms are the reading-room and the library. On the opposite side of the hall from the reading-room is Professor Raymond's recitation room. On the second floor of the main building are the recitation rooms of Professors Conant, Maginnis, Richardson, Dewey, Smith, and Kendrick. All these rooms are complete; have comfortable seats, window shades, carpets, etc. On the second floor of the main building is the trustees' room of the Education Society. The third and fourth stories of the main building are occupied by students. The rooms in the wing are principally occupied by students. In the wing is Professor Kendrick's valuable classical library. Professor Raymond, Dr. Conant, and others have libraries of more or less value in different rooms of the front building. The chapel is a light and pleasant room 70 feet long and 30 in width. On the east side is a carpeted rostrum. On the rostrum is a suitable reading-desk, and chairs for nine professors. Comfortable seats have been provided for the students, and for morning prayers and evening lectures no more convenient or appropriate chapel is needed for the present. The materials have been furnished for a geological cabinet, and a museum for whatever is rare and curious will soon be commenced. Rooms will be appropriated for both of these purposes."

The University itself never used the entire building. Under an arrangement made with the New York Baptist Union for Ministerial Education, which agreed to pay one-third of the rent of the building and of the wages of the janitor, the Rochester Theological Seminary was given the occupancy of four recitation rooms and what rooms were needed for its students. Besides, some other portions of the building and some of the things in it were used more or less in common.

Nor was this meant to be the permanent location of the University, for the trustees stated in their first report to the Regents that the University owned and would occupy the building "until its site is selected, and its intended buildings are erected."

It is also interesting at the present time, when measures are under way for the removal to Oak Hill of the College for Men, to note what an unidentified clipping shows that someone wrote about 1848 to a newspaper, when he understood that Madison University would be removed to Rochester. He said:

"Since the removal of this Institution to Rochester has been decided upon, considerable interest seems to be felt and expressed in regard to its particular locality. This is quite natural. The main edifice and the buildings necessarily connected with it, will undoubtedly be among the chief ornaments of the city; and particularly so, if they are erected in a becoming situation. . . . .

"In casting around for the situation of such a public edifice, it is as natural for the eye to look towards elevated ground as it is for the sunflower to follow the sun. . . . .

"On the southern boundary of the city stands a range of bold and picturesque hills, commencing on the bank of the Genesee and running eastward for more than a mile. These hills . . . . invite the erection of such buildings as those of this University. It has been predicted that Rochester is to be a city of colleges. If that be so, and we trust it will, this inevitably will be their location. . . . . The College Street of Rochester must occupy this beautiful hill. There is no other such fitting place. It seems raised up there for that glorious end. The Madison University may enjoy the honor of being first, but whether it does or not, that will yet be 'College Hill.' "

The *New York Recorder* of October 16, 1850, gives, in "Editorial Correspondence," some of the impressions made on Dr. Anderson by his first visit to Rochester, which he was able to make by stopping off while on his way to Brockport to attend a state convention of the Baptists. He said:

"After visiting its various points of interest, we were obliged to admit that in their eulogies the friends of Rochester had rigidly kept within the limits of truth. The city is spread over a large surface, leaving space for gardens and fruit trees, which give a remarkably rural and picturesque aspect to the entire place. The streets are wide, airy, and well paved and lighted. The unusually large number of cottage residences shows that the laboring portion of the population are to a great extent freeholders, while the dwellings of the wealthier inhabitants give evidence of a high degree of cultivation. For a city which has grown with such rapidity, the beauty and solidity of the private dwellings and public buildings are remarkable. The number of evangelical churches gives pleasing proof of the extent to which religion has been incorporated with the life of the place. . . . .

"We were of course curious to learn the accommodations which our friends had provided for the opening of the classes of the new University. The trustees have been peculiarly fortunate in securing the lease of a large and commodious building, just out of the business part of the city. It was originally erected for a hotel, but from a change in the location of the railroad station houses, it had become unprofitable for that purpose. . . . . The building . . . . contains accommodations for all the purposes of the University for years to come. It . . . . will furnish at once accommodations equal to those possessed by three-fourths of the colleges in the country. . . . .

"Orders have already been given for the importation of books from Europe to meet the demands of special departments of instruction. Apparatus sufficient for the immediate purposes of instruction is at the disposal of the teachers.

"We question whether a college has ever been started in our country with such facilities and advantages at the outset. Our friends are not

UNIVERSITY OF ROCHESTER

obliged to commence by laying out large sums in building before they can realize their subscription. Every necessary building is furnished to their hand. They have a faculty who have had long experience in instructing, ... whose reputation as scholars has for many years commanded the confidence of the literary and religious public. . . . .

"They are received gladly into the midst of an intelligent, wealthy, and moral community, situated in the midst of an agricultural country unsurpassed in its fertility and natural advantages by any territory on the face of the globe. With the favor of God, with the sympathy and prayers of the churches, the enterprise will succeed, and give the blessings of Christian education, of an able and cultivated ministry, to succeeding generations, who will rise up to invoke heaven's blessing on the memory of its self-sacrificing founders."

On September 17, 1850, which was the day after the Executive Board of the University of Rochester was created, that board appointed Judge Ira Harris, of Albany, "chancellor of the University till the president shall be elected."

The opening of the University was set by the trustees for the first Monday in November, 1850. That was the fourth. However, the opening exercises were held on Tuesday afternoon, the fifth.

Thus, "J.A.S.," who was probably Dr. Justin A. Smith, at that time pastor of the First Baptist Church, wrote to the New York *Recorder*, on November 6 (which was Wednesday):

"To most of your readers it will be gratifying to learn that the University of Rochester has this day commenced its regular routine of study and recitation. The exercises connected with the formal opening were held in the University chapel yesterday P.M., and were of a highly interesting character.

"The preliminary religious services were conducted by Dr. Kendrick [of the faculty]; Rev. H. W. Lee, of the St. Luke's Episcopal Church in this city; and Rev. J. B. Shaw, of the Second Presbyterian [or Brick] Church. In the absence of the Chancellor, ... Mr. John N. Wilder, president of the Board of Trustees, delivered the address. . . . . He was followed by E. Darwin Smith, Esq., a prominent lawyer in this city, who, in a handsome manner, expressed the cordiality with which the citizens of Rochester welcome the rising among them of this new Institution. Not a Baptist [but an Episcopalian] himself, he congratulated the denomination under whose fostering the University has reached a degree of maturity, that their endeavors have been crowned with results so pleasing.

UNIVERSITY OF ROCHESTER

The services were closed with prayer by Dr. Maginnis, singing the doxology, and the benediction by Rev. Alfred Bennett [a pioneer Baptist minister sometimes affectionately called "Father" Bennett].....

"Colleges and seminaries in New England, in our own state, in Canada, Nova Scotia, and New Brunswick have sent hither some of their choice students. Rochester and western New York are liberally represented, while the number who have come from rural sections show our country friends are willing to test the real advantages of a city location for students.....

"We know that when God prospers it is prosperity indeed; and, strongly assured that this which we behold is his doing, we look with confidence to the future, expecting large results of blessings to the world to follow the endowment and founding of the University of Rochester."

Likewise, the *Rochester Daily Democrat* of Wednesday morning, November 6, said that the opening exercises were held "at the chapel of the University, yesterday afternoon." It characterized them as "brief, but interesting," and gave the following description of them:

"The students who have already entered the Institution and a few citizens were present. After prayer by the Rev. Dr. Kendrick, reading of the

ROCHESTER AND COLGATE

Scriptures by Rev. Dr. Lee, and another prayer, by Rev. Mr. Shaw, an address to the students was made by John N. Wilder, Esq. . . . ."

Mr. Wilder's address, this report went on to say, was entirely of a practical character, intended to impress upon the students the great interest that was felt for them by the officers and faculty of the Institution, and the duty devolving upon them of seconding the efforts of their instructors and endeavoring by correct conduct to give character to the University. The espionage practiced in nearly all other colleges would not be instituted here. Those in charge started with the idea that all who came here to be taught and improve their minds were gentlemen, and they meant to treat them as such.

The instructors would not approach the students as proselyters; they were not employed for that purpose, and understood their position too well to try to proselyte. They came to do high service for a large body of Christians, by endeavoring in a noble and manly spirit to impart a Christian education to the young men intrusted to their care. While there would not be the least degree of sectarianism, the elements of a common Christianity would pervade and sanctify the whole course of instruction to be pursued.

UNIVERSITY OF ROCHESTER

Then Mr. Wilder made the somewhat surprising declaration, in view of all that was said during the removal controversy in favor of Rochester as a site for a collegiate institution, that "people had everywhere objected to the location of the college in a city—this being the only one, except that in the city of New York, so located." The speaker hoped, however, that the results of this enterprise would prove the wisdom of the location. He had confidence in Rochester, and believed that the religious element was strong here, and that the citizens were all anxious for the prosperity of the Institution.

"About sixty students," the *Daily Democrat* added, "have entered the University, and the number is expected to be increased. There are besides some twenty-five in the theological school.

"The appearance of the students is highly favorable, and the University has commenced its course most auspiciously."

On November 7, the Executive Board, at a "meeting held at the Greek recitation room," voted "that Rev. J. S. Maginnis be employed to instruct the Senior class in intellectual philosophy the present term, at the rate of $300 per year"; and, on November 28, "that the services of E. Peshine Smith [a lawyer, of Rochester] as teacher in mathematics be secured." The first catalogue of the University, issued some time in 1851, gave Mr. Smith as acting professor of mathematics and natural philosophy, and Dr. Maginnis as acting professor of intellectual and moral philosophy, while it had Thomas J. Conant, D.D., as professor of the Hebrew language and literature. Instruction in modern languages, it stated, was being given by professors in other departments. Albert H. Mixer was listed both as tutor and as librarian; whereas the *Annunciator* of January 1, 1851, reported as "Resident graduates: A. H. Mixer, Forestville; Oscar Howes, Carmel." James Noble was janitor.

The first faculty of the Rochester Theological Seminary consisted of Rev. John S. Maginnis, D.D., professor of biblical and pastoral theology, and Rev. Thomas J. Conant, D.D., professor of biblical criticism and interpretation; both of whom came from Madison University.

Not only did the University of Rochester and the Rochester Theological Seminary together take five members from the faculty of Madison University, and along with them a large proportion of the students of that University; but so many of its trustees had proposed to resign at one time that there would not have been a quorum left by which

UNIVERSITY OF ROCHESTER

could have been filled the vacancies thus created in the board—at least not without great difficulty. This led to a bargain being made whereby Madison University was given a reconstructed, satisfactory board. The consideration for this was a promise in writing by certain friends of that University that the professors who resigned in order to go to Rochester should by September 10 be paid the arrears in salaries due them, amounting in all to about $2,700, and that certain legal expenses which were due, not to exceed $625, should also be paid at an early date.

Of the thirteen trustees of Madison University who had been made trustees of the University of Rochester, six only resigned in 1850 from the board of Madison University: Friend Humphrey, Ira Harris, W. R. Williams, Seneca B. Burchard, Alonzo Wheelock, and James Edmunds. Those who still served on both boards were: William L. Marcy, John N. Wilder, Smith Sheldon, David R. Barton, Robert Kelly, Henry Tower, and John Munro. Henry Tower became the president of the board of Madison University, and in 1853 resigned from that of the University of Rochester.

On November 7, 1850, the Executive Board of the University of Rochester adopted the following rules relative to chapel exercises:

"First. The faculty is expected to be present.

"Second. The students are required to be present, and their absence noted by the faculty and reported to the board.

"Third. During prayer the students are to stand.

"Fourth. The services are to be short; not over ten minutes."

A resolution was passed by that board on November 28, "That Rev. A. C. Kendrick, Rev. Chester Dewey, and Rev. J. H. Raymond be requested to take charge of the chapel exercises till the appointment of a president." That was followed, December 2, by the adoption of a resolution that Professor A. C. Kendrick should be the chairman of the faculty "till the president is elected."

No organization of the students, the board further voted on December 2, would be allowed, unless the object and constitution of the society were approved by the faculty.

On December 9, 1850, Edwin Pancost tendered to the Executive Board his resignation as treasurer, and the office was given to William N. Sage, who for many years thereafter served as both secretary and treasurer.

On January 17, 1851, the Executive Board authorized its chairman "to purchase the University

UNIVERSITY OF ROCHESTER

Building now occupied, including a small lot on Elizabeth Street, for nine thousand dollars, or less; the time of payments to be made mutually satisfactory." This was followed, on March 8, by a resolution, "That we adopt as corporate seal of the University, till permanent seal is procured, the American half-dollar, and that the same be affixed to the bond and mortgage to be executed against the University building and land recently purchased."

Meanwhile (on February 17), the Executive Board passed a resolution which provided that three scholars annually should be selected from the public schools in the city of Rochester, in any manner that the Board of Education should designate, to receive gratuitous tuition during a full collegiate course in the University. That amounted, in the aggregate, to the establishment of twelve free scholarships.

The expenses of a student in the University were stated to be: tuition, per annum, $30; room rent, $4; incidental expenses, $6; while other necessary annual expenses, including board, washing, fuel, light, etc., might be estimated at $75, making a total of $115 for a year.

"Board," said the *Annunciator* of May 1, 1851, "can be obtained in good families for $1.50 per week; and board, washing, lodging, with furnished study-rooms, for from $2 to $2.25. A number of young men have been for some months past, and are still, boarding themselves at from 63 to 80 cents per week. They have food prepared and sent to their rooms."

The *Annunciator* of January 1, 1851, said that the University of Rochester, two months after its organization, with able professors and nearly seventy students, was working as perfectly and efficiently as if it had had years of growth and nurture. "Its mission is honorable, and will be glorious. Created to supply two great needs—one denominational, and the other local—it will admirably supply both."

Again, the *Annunciator* referred to the *New York Recorder* as having stated that, in a conversation upon the different systems of liberal education in this country, Dr. Humphrey, former president of Amherst College, gave that of the University of Rochester his decided preference. It was, in his view, the *model institution* of our country. It had made an advance on the systems theretofore acted upon by our American schools, but had avoided the error committed (as he conceived it) by some others, of adopting to an unwarranted extent the German plan.

UNIVERSITY OF ROCHESTER

At the close of the first term of the University of Rochester, "J.A.S." wrote to the *New York Recorder*, as appears in its number of January 1, 1851:

"We have completed the first in a series of academical periods, which are to be linked one to another, on and on—who shall say to what extent? .... We can now realize that a new University, on a basis unequalled in breadth and firmness, by any that has heretofore been laid by the Baptists of this country, is actually reared. Its machinery has been put in operation, and its several parts have been arranged, and fitted, and set to work; its students have assembled, received their first lessons, and a term is complete. .... What is the *foundation* of that fabric, whose stability and permanency are estimated? In one sense, it may be said that this foundation lies in the deep interest, the zealous affection of thousands, friends of religion and learning, who are the *founders* of this institution, and will be its patrons and supporters. .... The University of Rochester has in its professors, without exception, a treasure that is more to it than money could possibly become. .... The completeness of the organization; the perfect order and system that have prevailed from the very first day; the vigor that reigns; and, above all, the religious spirit that baptizes the whole; these are evidences that speak to the heart and confirm the hopes which more prominent appearances may have inspired."

Thus was the University of Rochester founded and auspiciously opened, leaving for further consideration the men to whom credit must be given for being its founders.

CHAPTER V

FOUNDERS OF THE UNIVERSITY OF ROCHESTER

No particular person can rightfully be called the founder of the University of Rochester. Neither can all those entitled to be termed its founders well be named. The *Annunciator* published, under the heading of "Founders of the University of Rochester," lists of subscribers numbering in the aggregate over eight hundred. It also distinctly declared, in June, 1850, with reference to the movement for the establishment of the University, that "no one man is necessary to its success." Nevertheless it is easy to see in certain names, which have been mentioned with more or less frequency, those of some of the founders, and even to distinguish among them the names of some of the more important leaders of the movement or movements which finally culminated in the founding of the University. However, no attempt will be made here either to describe or to list, even very briefly, more than a few of the leaders of special interest.

One man who was clearly a leader and, taking all in all, the greatest worker among the founders of the University of Rochester, was John Nichols Wilder. He had been a merchant in Albany and had received from an uncle what was then regarded as a large legacy, after which he appears to have in a great measure devoted his time, talents, and means to aiding benevolent enterprises and promoting higher education, especially for the Baptist denomination, to which he belonged. This helps to explain why he entered into and worked for the removal plan as he did and, after that was checked, for the establishment of the University of Rochester. Moreover, not only did he work diligently within the denomination to promote those enterprises, but he also did a great deal to get assistance for them from men outside the denomination. His subscription for the University of Rochester was by much the largest one, even though subsequent adverse circumstances and his early death appear to have prevented, according to certain records, more than $5,635 being realized on the subscription, which was originally for $10,000, payable in ten annual instalments.

So much interest did Mr. Wilder take in the establishment of the University of Rochester that, after a time, he moved to Rochester and lived there for a while. His high appreciation of the city as a site for a University was undoubtedly to some

FOUNDERS OF ROCHESTER

extent gained from visits which he had made to relatives who resided in Rochester.

Mr. Wilder had not himself enjoyed the advantages of a collegiate education. Nevertheless, he had in such measure made up for the lack of it that, at a regular meeting, on July 14, 1852, of the trustees of the University of Rochester (the official minutes state): "After a full and free discussion of the subject of a financial and executive head of the University, John N. Wilder was unanimously elected president, the compensation to be twelve hundred dollars per year. On motion, Chancellor Harris and Hon. William L. Marcy were appointed a committee to wait upon Mr. Wilder and inform him of his appointment as president." However, he declined to accept the office, one explanation being that he had previously entered into other important engagements of a business nature.

One of the special features of the Commencement program of 1857 was the delivery by Mr. Wilder, before the literary societies, of a long, original poem, entitled "Rochester." The poem not only contained noble sentiment and classic references, but also abounded in puns and witty allusions of local interest. It was afterward published in book form.

In 1858, Mr. Wilder delivered before citizens of

ROCHESTER AND COLGATE

Albany a patriotic Fourth-of-July poem, two lines of which were:

"Love well your country—in no duty lag,
Stand by its altars and stand by its flag."

Mr. Wilder was born in Pittston, Maine. He died suddenly, from apoplexy, at Albany, New York, on July 15, 1858, aged 44 years. "The stores were generally closed at the time of his funeral."

The *Albany Argus* said of him that "he was extensively known, and his genial and excellent qualities made him as extensively beloved. John N. Wilder was no ordinary man. He had intellect, genius, cultivation, literary taste, and social gifts, in liberal endowment."

In the *Examiner*, of New York, of July 21, 1859, a correspondent, referring to the commemorative discourse which had been delivered on the twelfth by President Anderson, stated that Mr. Wilder's rare combination of business capacity and intellectual culture and talent, rising even to genius; his unwonted and marvelous rapidity of thought, united with great coolness and caution in action; his delicate appreciation of whatever was graceful and profound in art and literature; his extraordinary mastery of racy, idiomatic, and elegant English, both in writing and speaking; and finally, his

FOUNDERS OF ROCHESTER

genial social qualities, and his exemplary domestic and Christian virtues, were discriminatingly and truthfully portrayed. Moreover, Dr. Anderson said that to Mr. Wilder "belonged, beyond all others, the honor of founding this seat of learning."

To similar effect was this one of the series of resolutions which the Executive Board of the University adopted on July 16, 1858, after having been informed of the death of Mr. Wilder:

"*Resolved*, That the sagacity, energy, and courage which he brought to bear on this enterprise, when it existed only in idea, and the zeal with which he continued to labor on in its behalf during his entire life, entitle him to the foremost rank among that noble body of men who laid the foundation of this seat of learning."

Another great worker with voice and pen, for about ten months from the commencement of the campaign for the removal of Madison University to Rochester, or until he changed his residence from Rochester to Boston, was Rev. Pharcellus Church, D.D. As described in Cathcart's *Baptist Encyclopaedia*, he was a man of noble intellect, splendid culture, a great heart, saintly piety, and unsullied record. One of the products of his pen treated of *The Cause and Cure of Religious Dissensions;* and in 1846 he was sent as a delegate of

ROCHESTER AND COLGATE

Rochester churches to a world-conference in London called to establish an Evangelical Alliance or Christian Union. Still, in his zeal for the removal plan, he became more or less unpleasantly involved in bitter controversy, of which there was not a little at different times, especially in correspondence published in some of the denominational and local papers. Then, on Christmas Day, 1847, Dr. Church wrote to the *New York Recorder:*

"Hamilton . . . . has its memories that will never die. It has been the home of those whom my heart cherishes with more than filial love and veneration. Their sepulchers will forever stand as mementoes of departed worth—and of the beginning of a great educational history. The Lord preserve us from hurting the oil or the wine. If the object for which these men lived and died cannot be better secured at Rochester than at Hamilton, God hold us back from attempting its removal. Oh, that we could acquire . . . . the habit of crucifying all local, all party, and all personal feelings; that we may merge our whole being in God and in the greatest good."

The removal enterprise seemed naturally, immediately after it was suggested, to center in the First Baptist Church of Rochester, where it found, besides Dr. Church, other strong, active advocates

FOUNDERS OF ROCHESTER

in a number of the leading members of the church.

One of the latter was Deacon Oren Sage (1787–1866), who, born in Middletown, Connecticut, where his paternal ancestor from Wales settled in 1652, came to Rochester in 1827. Deacon Sage was a man of strong character and sense of right combined with a spirit of kindness and patience. He was highly regarded and of great influence, not only in the church, of which he was a deacon and a trustee, but outside of it as well. He knew the value to young men of a liberal education, perhaps all the more because he himself had never had the benefit of one. In consequence, he was for years closely identified with the activities of the Baptist Education Society of the State of New York. Then, from the time of the first meeting relative to the removal of Madison University to Rochester until the University of Rochester was founded, he worked arduously in the attempt to secure the former, and afterward in what was done to found the latter, as things that ought to be achieved. Especially did he do more than anyone else, except perhaps Mr. Wilder, toward getting the earlier subscriptions that encouraged and made possible the founding of the University. But after the University was founded he turned his attention chiefly to helping to sustain the Rochester Theological Seminary.

ROCHESTER AND COLGATE

William Nathan Sage (1819-90), a son of Deacon Oren Sage, was another zealous and effective worker in the University cause, from its inception. When he was twelve years of age he joined the First Baptist Church of Rochester. As time passed, he became a teacher in the Sunday school, then superintendent of the school, and eventually a deacon in the church. He was graduated from Brown University in 1840. For a number of years he was a bookseller and publisher. In 1855-58 he was county clerk. Subsequently he succeeded his father in what then became the firm of Pancost, Sage & Co., sometimes described as manufacturers of boots and shoes, and sometimes as dealers in boots, shoes, and leather. Besides, he was one of the organizers and the president of a safe deposit company, became the president of a savings bank, and rendered valuable service in other responsible positions. But most important of all for present consideration, for practically forty years he was a trustee and the secretary of the Board of Trustees of the University of Rochester, as well as its treasurer.

In a paper which, in 1881, he read before the Board of Trustees of the University, in connection with his annual report as treasurer, he said:

"The labor performed during these years by your treasurer has not been light, and it has cost him sacrifice to fulfil the duties imposed. Many and urgent invitations, with pecuniary inducements, have been presented, that might have been attractive under other circumstances, but they have failed to draw him from his post of duty, or to compromise him as the guardian of trust funds; and he has now the privilege of saying that not one dollar of the funds of the University invested by himself, or by his advice, has been lost during all these years, while many of the investments have appreciated in value, from 5 to 25 per cent, when paid, over what they cost. The receipted bills of thirty years are saved and filed and ready for examination at any time. . . . .

"The faculty have always been paid their salaries when due, with exceptional instances where interest was added for the delay; and sometimes the personal indorsement of the treasurer has been used for from $6,000 to $10,000, to secure promptness to those needing their just dues. His own salary was fixed at the close of the first year's services at $600, and, on account of poverty of income, has never been raised in the four to six advances to the other officers, so that, after paying bookkeeper and some other expenses, but little remained personal to himself. . . . . His traveling and other expenses while absent on University business, with the exception of two or three visits to New York, have never been mentioned or charged. . . . .

"More glory might have been earned had he given $50,000 in money to the University than in substantially giving the same amount in a kind of service that money cannot always purchase. But when he has seen colleges and universities shipwrecked by financial mismanagement, even where the instruction has been comparatively good, you will pardon your treasurer for feeling proud of having been connected with a University that has triumphed in both departments."

Dr. Martin B. Anderson, while president of the University, once said that "the first twenty years of growth and prosperity on the part of the University were greatly due to the skill, judgment, and self-sacrificing labor of William N. Sage."

Edwin Pancost (1812–67) was related to the Sages by marriage, and, like them, was prominent in the First Baptist Church, in which he was a deacon, besides being one of its trustees. At the age of nineteen, with a common-school education, he left the farm and went to Rochester to engage in business. He became very successful as a manufacturer of boots and shoes, especially after forming, with Deacon Oren Sage, a partnership for conducting the business under the firm name of Sage and Pancost. In addition to that, he became a trustee of one bank and a director of another. He had a studious and independent mind, also high social qualities. For several years he was an efficient member of the Board of Education of the city of Rochester. He was one of the active early supporters of the removal movement, and afterward of that for founding the University of Rochester. That his ability and the services which he rendered up to the time that the University was provisionally chartered, and could render it thereafter, were appreciated, was evidenced by his being made a trustee and a member of the Executive Board of the University, as well as its first treasurer, although he soon relinquished that office in order that it might be joined to that of secretary, as a matter of convenience and economy.

Worthy co-workers with these men who were foremost among the members of the First Baptist Church in doing what was done to bring about the founding of the University of Rochester, were two similarly substantial members of the Second Baptist Church of Rochester. They were Deacon David R. Barton and Elon Huntington, both of whom were trustees of the church, men of sagacity, successful in business, and influential in church and

ROCHESTER AND COLGATE

community. Both, too, were among the first trustees appointed for the University, and were chosen members of its Executive Board.

David R. Barton was a manufacturer of and dealer in edge tools. In 1847, he was elected a trustee of Madison University, and so remained until 1852, when he resigned. As a trustee of the University of Rochester, his service extended over more than twenty years.

Elon Huntington was born in Vermont, in 1808. He attended district schools until, at sixteen years of age, he himself became the teacher in one. In 1837 he settled in Rochester, where he engaged in various business enterprises, and became the cashier of a bank. As he lived until 1899, he was for some time known as being the sole survivor of the original trustees of the University of Rochester. It was said of him that for forty-five years or more he never missed one of the regular meetings of the Board of Trustees, or failed to attend every one of the Commencements of the University.

Various other Baptists of Rochester did all that they reasonably could do toward the founding of the University. One of them in particular, was Alvah Strong, who had more than a personal influence, being one of the publishers of the *Rochester Daily Democrat*. However, after the University

FOUNDERS OF ROCHESTER

was founded, he turned his personal attention for the most part to aiding in firmly establishing and maintaining the Rochester Theological Seminary.

While the founding of the University of Rochester was essentially a Baptist enterprise, promoted under Baptist leadership, many public-spirited citizens of Rochester of other denominations contributed materially to it. Partly in recognition of this fact, three of the men who were made the first trustees of the University were residents of Rochester who were not Baptists, namely, Frederick Whittlesey, William Pitkin, and Everard Peck. Mr. Whittlesey and Mr. Pitkin were Episcopalians, the former being a vestryman, and the latter a warden in St. Luke's Episcopal Church. Mr. Peck was a Presbyterian.

The support that the Episcopalians of Rochester gave to the Baptists is partially shown by the fact that at the annual convention of the Episcopalians of western New York, which was held at Geneva in August, 1848, it was explained that no subscription had been obtained in Rochester for the Hobart Professorship in Geneva College, "owing to an effort which was then being made in Rochester for another Institution"—the removal of Madison University to Rochester, subscriptions having been made for the latter, in part "in consideration of the local advantages it would afford."

Frederick Whittlesey (1799–1852) was born in Connecticut, was graduated from Yale College in 1818, and was admitted to the bar in 1821. In 1822 he became a resident of Rochester. He was once treasurer of Monroe County, was four years in Congress, eight years a vice-chancellor, and one year a justice of the Supreme Court of the State of New York. It was said of him that he was a "profound lawyer; a gentleman of extensive reading, retentive memory, and sound judgment"; a man who was "universally respected." He took a special interest in helping to promote and maintain educational and other institutions for the public benefit. Not only was he made one of the first trustees of the University of Rochester, but he was elected vice-president of the Board of Trustees, and a member of the Executive Board.

In 1836, the boundaries of the city of Rochester were "extended so as to include, within the limits thereof, the farm of William Pitkin, situated in the town of Brighton," and all the land lying between his farm and what was theretofore the eastern boundary of the city. Mr. Pitkin subsequently became a wholesale and retail druggist, and one of the leading citizens of Rochester. In 1845–46, he was the mayor of the city. In 1852, he was elected vice-president of the Board of Trustees and a member of the Executive Board of the University of Rochester, to fill vacancies caused by the death of Mr. Whittlesey.

Everard Peck has been described as having been a "Connecticut Yankee" and a man of strong character, who left a favorable mark on everything with which he had to do. He became a resident of Rochester in 1816, and thereafter engaged in business as a bookseller, printer, and bookbinder. On July 7, 1818, he launched the *Rochester Telegraph*, "Pledg'd to Religion, Liberty, and Law," declaring: "To sit down in silent apathy, is not our duty or our object. We cannot submit to that temporary policy which looks at vice and folly with silent indifference." On September 6, 1825, he announced the turning over of the publication of the paper to Thurlow Weed, who had for some time assisted him in its management. Mr. Peck, it has been said, aided materially in the founding of the University of Rochester. His wife was a sister of John N. Wilder.

Rev. Sewall S. Cutting, D.D., was one of the Baptists in New York City who did a great deal toward the founding of the University of Rochester. He was a man of genial disposition and exceptional ability, a fine scholar, clear thinker, and an accomplished writer, who had been graduated with high honors from the University of Vermont. For a number of years he exerted a wide and strong influence in the Baptist denomination as the editor of the *New York Recorder* (until Martin B. Anderson, who had, with James S. Dickerson, D.D., purchased the paper, succeeded him as its editor, in June, 1850). In 1855, Dr. Cutting was elected professor of rhetoric and history in the University of Rochester, and held that position until 1868, when he resigned it, in order to become the secretary of the American Baptist Educational Commission.

Rev. William R. Williams, D.D., LL.D. (1804–85), was another early and strong champion, in New York City, of the University of Rochester. He was of Welsh descent, was graduated from Columbia College in 1822, and was admitted to the bar in 1826. After practicing law for several years, he turned to the ministry in 1831, and was for more than half a century the pastor of the Amity Street Baptist Church. That, like himself, had a distinct individuality, the "meeting-house," as it was commonly called by the members of the church, being very plain, although built of marble, while the congregation was not overlarge, but one responsive to a reverent, simple, and scholarly

FOUNDERS OF ROCHESTER

ministry. It was said that a plainer, more unassuming possessor of genius and learning than Dr. Williams it would be difficult to find, and that when he closed the Bible one felt that he had delivered a message from on high. Nor did he have religious prejudices; instead, he appreciated the great and good of all times. He was one of the incorporators and first trustees of Madison University, and also of the University of Rochester. A printed catalogue of his library was issued to aid in its sale at auction, in 1896. The catalogue was in two parts: one of 317 pages and 4,256 numbers, and the other of 136 pages and 2,079 numbers. The library was described as being composed of "a very large and varied collection of books and pamphlets gathered during many years of study and research into the ecclesiastical and religious controversies of former times, including many scarce works specially relating to the celebrated Jansenist controversy, the Jesuits, their doctrines and practices, the Mennonites, Baptists, etc."

Robert Kelly, LL.D. (1808–56), a trustee of the University and the chairman of the committee which produced the "Plan of Instruction," was born in New York City, of Scotch Presbyterian parentage. After the death of Robert's mother, his father married a woman of strong nonconformist, Baptist antecedents. One effect of this was that Robert Kelly, although he never joined any church, became greatly attached to the Baptists, worked with them in many ways as if one of them, and for many years attended the Amity Street Baptist Church, he and Dr. Williams becoming close friends and fellow-workers in divers causes. In his fourteenth year, Robert entered Columbia College at the head of his class, and by hard work and strict application maintained that position until his graduation in 1826. He and his two brothers inherited (from their father) a dry-goods business, from which, in 1837, he was able to retire with a competence and thereafter devote considerable attention to the promotion of educational and other interests for the general welfare, to further some of which he did not hold aloof from politics. The *Annunciator* of June 20, 1850, said of him:

"Mr. Kelly is a gentleman to whom the Baptist denomination will ever be indebted. He has been for some years one of the Board of Trustees of Madison University. In the preparatory labor of establishing the University of Rochester he has shared largely. His position in New York shows that at home he is properly appreciated. . . . . We have but one objection to Mr. Kelly, i.e., he is rather too stringent in his business habits. The rapidity with which he executes, and the tenacity with which he holds on, is rather wearying to gentlemen somewhat gray and very plethoric."

At a joint meeting of the Executive Board and the Faculty of Instruction, resolutions offered by President Anderson were adopted, stating that in the death of Mr. Kelly the University of Rochester had "lost one of its most distinguished founders and most active, constant and intelligent friends; and the cause of education in the state of New York, one of its wisest and most vigorous promoters"; that in him was recognized "an eminent example for the philanthropist, the scholar, and the Christian; a man whose career and attainments were an illustrious proof of the compatibility of the most successful cultivation of science and letters with the highest capacity in the administration of affairs."

Like these trustees, the other original trustees of the University, and many other men who aided in founding it, were men of interesting personalities and achievements which might well be noted here. Still, the foregoing biographical sketches will, perhaps, without any more, sufficiently indicate the kind of men who were the leaders among those who, through labors together, and with their subscriptions, founded the University of Rochester.

INDEX

INDEX

Academy, Hamilton, 25
Address, 71, 72
Albany, 46, 50, 64, 89, 105; Baptist Education Society, 82; Erie Canal from, to Buffalo, 3; railroads, 24
Albany Argus, 148
Albany Evening Journal, 81
Allegany County, 13
Allen, Justice W. F., 84
Allen Street Seminary, 9
Allen's Creek, 8
Amherst College, 142
Amity Street Baptist Church, 67, 160, 162
Anderson Hall, iii
Anderson, Martin B., 123, 148, 149, 154, 163
Annals of the Baptist Pulpit, 91
Annunciator, 112, 113, 114, 128, 138, 141, 142, 145, 162
Assembly, Journal of the, 37, 81
Auburn Daily Advertiser, 62

Babcock, Benjamin W., 81
Backus, J. S., 101, 102
Bainbridge, Rev., 51
Baptist church: at Eaton, 31; at Hamilton, 23, 27, 28; at Rochester, 46, 49, 52, 116, 150

Baptist Education Society of the State of New York, 26, 29, 30, 40, 42, 68, 81, 85, 151
Baptist Missionary Convention, 26
Baptist Register, Utica, 30, 31, 69, 92, 103
Baptist Theological Seminary, 29. See Hamilton Literary and Theological Institution
Baptists, 8, 15, 16, 25, 91, 96; control of theological instruction by, 101; denomination, 76; Educational Convention of, 82, 108

Barton, D. R., 52, 54, 59, 60, 105, 107, 118, 139, 155, 156
Beardsley, Henry G., 81
Beebe, A. M., 101
Bennett, Rev. Alfred, 83; "Father," 135
Boardman, E., 51
Bond, Senator Thomas H., 88
Brackett, A. J., 60
Bright, Edward, Jr., 40
Brighton Plank Road, 7, 8
Brown, General Theron, 72
Brown University, 28, 122, 152
Bucknell University, 30
Buffalo, 3, 64, 65, 92; University of Western New York at, 13
Buffalo Courier, 62

ROCHESTER AND COLGATE

Burbank, David, 72
Burbank, G. W., 52, 105
Burchard, Theodore, 81
Burchard, Seneca B., 40, 108, 139
Burrows, R. G., 102
Burrows, Roswell S., 83, 108, 118
Butts, Isaac, 59

Caldwell, Joseph, 40
Camp, Harman (Harmon), 14
Candid Appeal, A, 66, 67, 71, 76
Capwell, Deacon P., 72
Case, Rev. Z., 53
Cayuga County, 13
Chapin, Moses, 14
Charter 14, 15, 104, 105; failure to obtain, 39; "provisional," 106, 117; resolution approving, 18; to Rochester, 103, 108
Chenango Canal, 24
Chenango County, 39
Chenango River, 25
Chenango Valley, 25, 77
Cheney, William H., 51, 105
Child's Building, 5
Church, Pharcellus, 40, 46, 50, 51, 52, 53, 59, 60, 65, 71, 72, 91, 149
Clinton (Hamilton) College, 21
Cobb, William, 40, 83
Colby (Waterville) College, 28
Colgate, William, 40, 68, 83
Colgate University, 32. *See* Hamilton Literary and Theological Institution *and* Madison University

Columbia (King's) College, 11, 160
Columbian College (George Washington University), 29, 39
Committee of Nine, 102, 105, 106
Conant, Rev. Thomas J., 41, 116, 118, 128, 138
Cone, Rev. S. H., 83
Cook, Henry, 59
Cottage Edifice, 44
Curtis, George, 40
Cutting, Sewall S., 103, 159

Daniels, H., 72
Davis, George R., 105
Davis, Henry, 101, 102
Dean, Dr. Henry W., 49, 54
Degrees: at Columbian College, 39; at Rochester, 126
Dewey, Dr. Chester, 59, 60, 116, 118, 128, 140
Dickerson, J. S., 160
Doolittle, J. R., 72
Dwight, Henry, 14, 94
Dwinelle, J. W., 59

East Avenue, 8
Eastern Edifice, 32, 44
Eaton, Rev. George W., 41, 87
Edmonds, James, 40, 108, 111, 112, 139
Educational Convention: at Albany, 82; at Rochester, 108
Edwards, Harvey, 40
Elliot, Jesse, 72

[168]

INDEX

Ely, W. W., 59
Episcopalians, 157
Erie Canal, 3, 4; connected with Susquehanna River, 24

Fisber (Fisher), Nathaniel W., 14
Founders, 145, 146, 163. *See* University of Rochester
Free Academy, 122
Freeman, 112

Genesee River, 2, 4
Genesee County, 13
Geneva (Hobart) College, 11, 55, 91, 157
George Washington University (Columbian College), 29
Gibbons, Washington, 59
Graves, Amos, 40
Graves, Samuel, 42
Gridley, Justice Philo, 84, 85, 86, 87
Griffin, Ebenezer, 59

Hall, Albert G., 14
Hamilton, 63, 71; education in, 25, 37; incorporated, 24; population of, in 1847, 24; railroads, 24; Theological Seminary, 27, 85; village of, 23, 24, 37, 45
Hamilton Academy, 25
Hamilton Baptist Missionary Society, 25, 28
Hamilton College (at Clinton), 11, 21, 73
Hamilton Democratic Reflector, 90
Hamilton Literary and Theological Institution, 27, 29, 30, 31, 32, 46, 65, 103; admission to, 34, 35; Collegiate Department, 37; departments of, 33; expenses at, 34; first catalogue of, 33; growth of, 37, 45; incorporation of, 38; rules of, 35, 36; site of, 32. *See* Colgate University *and* Madison University.

Hamilton, S., 59
Hamilton University, bill to incorporate, 38. *See* Madison University
Harmon, Elisha, 53, 72
Harmon, General Rawson, 72
Harmon, Rawson, Jr., 108
Harris, Ira, 40, 102, 105, 107, 139, 147
Harvard University, 20
Hascall, Daniel, 27, 31, 84, 87
Herrington, Rev., 51
"Hill," the, 32
Hills, Isaac, 59
Hobart College, 11. *See* Geneva College
Hodge, Rev. J. L., 68
Holland, Rev. F. W., 18, 59, 60
Hopkins, Asa T., 14
Hotchkiss, V. R., 102, 108
Howard, Deacon D., 72
Humphrey, Friend, 40, 83, 105, 107, 139
Huntington, Elon, 51, 52, 54, 60, 105, 107, 118, 155, 156

Journal of the Assembly, 37, 81
Journal of the Senate, 13

Kelly, Robert, 40, 80, 102, 107, 116, 122, 123, 139, 161
Kempshall, Thomas, 59
Kendrick, Asahel C., 116, 118, 128, 134, 140
Kendrick, Rev. Nathaniel, 31, 32, 40, 41, 118
King's College, 11. *See* Columbia College

Lake Missionary Society, 25
Lathrop, Leonard, 14
Laws of Hamilton Literary and Theological Institution, 35
Lee, Charles M., 14, 15
Lee, Rev. H. W., 134
Libraries, 5
Lima, Methodist school at, 21
Livingston County, 13
Luckey, Rev. Samuel, 14, 18, 59

Mack, I. E., 59
Madison College, bill to incorporate, 39
Madison County, 23, 37, 38, 39
Madison University, 1, 23, 95; Baptist trustees of, 46; buildings of, 51; catalogue of, 42; charter of, 46; now Colgate, 1; endowment of, 48, 53, 64, 65, 67, 69, 78, 97; financial problem of, 47; first honorary degree conferred by, 46; future of, 94; incorporation of, 40; location of, 40, 71, 77; organization of, 41; professors in, 118, 138; registration at, 41; relief of, 93; removal of, 22, 49, 50, 52, 53, 54, 55, 57, 59, 61, 64, 65, 69, 76, 78, 87; report to Regents of, 41; suits against, 84, 103; trustees of, 41, 47, 79, 100, 139
Madison University, The First Half-Century of, 88
Maginnis, Rev. John S., 41, 88, 89, 90, 91, 128, 135, 137, 138
Maine Literary and Theological Institution, 28
Mann, Alexander, 57, 59
Marcy, William L., 40, 105, 107, 139, 147
Matthews, Selah, 14, 15
Mechanics' Literary Association, 5; Rochester Athenaeum and, 9
Metcalf, Rev. W., 49, 51
Middlebury College, 27
Mixer, Albert H., 138
Monroe County, 13, 52, 158; Baptists in, 56
Mount Hope Botanic Garden and Nursery, 6
Mount Hope Cemetery, 6
Munro, John, 40, 108, 139
Museum, of Rochester, The, 5

New York: academies in, 11; College of the City of, 122; Regents of the University of the State of, 11 (*see* Regents); state of, 11
New York Baptist Union for Ministerial Education, 109, 116, 129

[170]

INDEX

New York Recorder, 63, 71, 96, 103, 109, 123, 131, 135, 142, 143, 150, 160
New York & Erie Railroad, 77

Oak Hill, 130
Oliver, William M., 14
Oneida County, 39
Onondaga County, 25
Ontario County, 13

Paine, N. E., 59, 60
Palmyra, 13
Pancost, Edwin, 51, 107, 117, 118, 140, 154
Payne, Elisha, 23
Payne, Samuel, 23, 26, 32
Paynesville, 23
Peck, Everard, 59, 107, 118, 157, 159
Perkins, W. H., 59
Perrin, Darius, 59
Pierce, Alva, 40
Pitkin, William, 10, 60, 107, 157, 158
Plainfield, 24
Plan of Instruction, 119, 125, 161
Pomeroy, Enos, 14, 15
Pond, Elias, 59
Porter, Albert H., 14
Porter, Samuel D., 59
Presbyterian (Brick) Church, 14
Putnam, Joseph, 59

Railroads: Auburn and Rochester, 8; building of, 3; Tonawanda, 8

Raymond, J. H., 41, 96, 116, 118, 140
Raymond, Rev. R. R., 58, 102, 108
Regents of the University of the State of New York, 11, 12, 41, 98, 105, 106, 126
Remonstrance, The, 89
Richardson, J. F., 41, 118, 128
Rochester: banks in, 8; Baptists of, 52; churches in, 6, 8; city of, 1, 5, 6, 13; city of colleges, 131; city directory, 5, 7, 8; and Colgate University, 1; commercial industry in, 4, 7; completion of bridge at, 3; development of, 3; early settlers, 4; educational institutions in, 9, 64; the "Falls," 3; "Flour City" and "Flower City," 3, 4; free high school in, 9, 10; incorporation of, 3, 24; increases in area of, 3; libraries in, 5; manufacturing in, 6; newspapers in, 6, 20; places of amusement, 5; plank roads, 7; population of, at various dates, 1; public schools in, 5, 6; railroads, 3, 8; religion in, 4, 8; removal of Madison University to, 49, 60, 63, 64, 78, 87, 99; "Rochesterville," 3; seeds, 4; site of, 1, 2; University at, 14, 15, 60; water-power, 2, 3, 4
Rochester and Charlotte Plank Road, 7, 8
Rochester City Garden, 6
Rochester Collegiate Institute, 9, 10

[171]

ROCHESTER AND COLGATE

Rochester, Colonel Nathaniel, 2
Rochester Daily Advertiser, 20
Rochester Daily American, 20, 57, 58, 60
Rochester Daily Democrat, 6, 16, 19, 57, 60, 91, 135; Alvah Strong, publisher, 21, 156
Rochester Female Academy, 9
Rochester, Henry E., 15, 59
Rochester Institution of General Education, 10
Rochester Institute of Practical Education, 10, 11
Rochester *Telegraph*, 159
Rochester Theological Seminary, 109, 111, 129, 138, 151, 157
Rogers, Medad, 84

Sage, Oren, 53, 60, 65, 105, 111, 140, 151, 152, 154
Sage, William N., 54, 72, 83, 107, 113, 117, 118, 152, 154
Seminaries, 5, 9, 27, 34
Seminary, Mrs. Greenough's, 9
Senate, Journal of the, 13
Seward Female Seminary, 9
Shaw, James B., 14, 60, 134
Sheldon, Smith, 40, 107, 139
Shepard, E., 59
Skaneateles, 24
Skinner, John B., 14
Smith, A. G., 52, 105
Smith, E. Darwin, 14, 15, 134
Smith, E. Peshine, 59, 137
Smith, Elijah F., 107
Smith, Justin A., 134

Smith, L. Ward, 59
Spear, P. B., 51, 88
Stanwood, Rev. H., 51, 53
Stilwell, H., 59
Stimson, Rev. H. K., 51, 53
Stone, Marcena, 10
Strong, Alvah, 21, 54, 94, 111, 156
Strong, Augustus H., 111
Susquehanna River, 24
Syracuse, city of, 63, 64, 78
Syracuse Journal, 56, 58
Syracuse Star, 6

Taylor, E. E. L., 101
Townsend, Palmer, 40, 67, 83
Tower, Henry, 40, 83, 102, 103, 108, 139
Tracy, Phineas L., 14
Trevor, Joseph, 40
Trustees, Board of: denominational majority, 18; of Madison University, 41, 47, 79, 100; of Rochester University, 16, 94, 100
Tucker, Elisha, 40
Tucker, Rev. Levi, 65

Union College, 11
United States Hotel Building, iii, 119, 126
University of the City of New York, 11
University of the State of New York, Regents of, 11
University of Western New York, 13, 16, 20, 64

INDEX

University of Rochester, 60, 83, 105, 107, 114; admission to, 105; and Colgate, v; collegiate and theological departments of, 100; endowment of, 20, 60, 107, 117; first catalogue of, 125, 138; first faculty of, 138; first trustees of, 14; founders of, 145; founding of, v, 1, 15, 99, 144; funds for, 110, 112; incorporation of, 14; instruction in, 17, 125; need for, 16; non-sectarian, 16, 17, 19, 21, 92; opening of, 133, 134; plan of instruction of, 17, 119; plan of organization of, 101; Presbyterian incorporators of, 15, 21; removal of Madison University sought, 99; scholarships in, 116; site, 129, 130; students in, 135, 137; subjects taught, 120; trustees of, 93, 100, 107, 117, 139, 157, 158

Utica, 63, 64, 78; railroad, 24; roads, 24

Utica Gazette, 61

Wadsworth, James S., 14

Walker, Charles, 40

Watchman and Reflector, Boston, 110

Water-power of Rochester, 2, 3, 4

Waterville (Colby) College, 28

Wayland, Dr. Francis, 74, 122

Weed, Thurlow, 159

Welch, Bartholomew T., 40

Western Edifice, 32, 44

Westcott, Rev. Isaac, 101

Wheelock, Alonzo, 40, 67, 100, 108, 139

Whittlesey, Frederick, 10, 59, 107, 116, 117, 118, 127, 157, 158

Wilder, John N., 40, 50, 51, 53, 57, 59, 66, 75, 82, 90, 102, 105, 107, 111, 117, 118, 134, 139, 146, 147, 148, 159, 160

Williams, Gibbon, 71

Williams, William R., 40, 67, 68, 69, 71, 83, 108, 116, 139

Winants, H. L., 59

Yates County, 13